The Encyclopedia of
Collectibles

Other Publications:

The Seafarers

The Great Cities

World War II

Home Repair and Improvement

The World's Wild Places

The Time-Life Library of Boating

Human Behavior

The Art of Sewing

The Old West

The Emergence of Man

The American Wilderness

The Time-Life Encyclopedia of Gardening

Life Library of Photography

This Fabulous Century

Foods of the World

Time-Life Library of America

Time-Life Library of Art

Great Ages of Man

Life Science Library

The Life History of the United States

Time Reading Program

Life Nature Library

Life World Library

Family Library:
   How Things Work in Your Home
   The Time-Life Book of the Family Car
   The Time-Life Family Legal Guide
   The Time-Life Book of Family Finance

The Encyclopedia of
Collectibles

Folk Art to Horse-drawn Carriages

TIME-LIFE BOOKS, ALEXANDRIA, VIRGINIA

Time-Life Books Inc.
is a wholly owned subsidiary of
TIME INCORPORATED

FOUNDER: Henry R. Luce 1898-1967

Editor-in-Chief: Hedley Donovan
Chairman of the Board: Andrew Heiskell
President: James R. Shepley
Vice Chairmen: Roy E. Larsen, Arthur Temple
Corporate Editors: Ralph Graves,
Henry Anatole Grunwald

TIME-LIFE BOOKS INC.
Managing Editor: Jerry Korn
Executive Editor: David Maness
Assistant Managing Editors: Dale M. Brown,
Martin Mann, John Paul Porter
Art Director: Tom Suzuki
Chief of Research: David L. Harrison
Director of Photography: Robert G. Mason
Planning Director: Thomas Flaherty (acting)
Senior Text Editor: Diana Hirsh
Assistant Art Director: Arnold C. Holeywell
Assistant Chief of Research: Carolyn L. Sackett
Assistant Director of Photography: Dolores A. Littles

Chairman: Joan D. Manley
President: John D. McSweeney
Executive Vice Presidents: Carl G. Jaeger,
John Steven Maxwell, David J. Walsh
Vice Presidents: Peter G. Barnes (Comptroller),
Nicholas Benton (Public Relations),
John L. Canova (Sales), Nicholas J. C. Ingleton
(Asia), James L. Mercer (Europe/South Pacific),
Herbert Sorkin (Production), Paul R. Stewart
(Promotion)
Personnel Director: Beatrice T. Dobie
Consumer Affairs Director: Carol Flaumenhaft

The Encyclopedia of Collectibles
Chief Researcher: Phyllis K. Wise
Researchers: Mary G. Burns, Ann Dusel Kuhns,
Trudy W. Pearson, Judith W. Shanks
Editorial Assistant: Jane S. Hanna

Editorial Production
Production Editor: Douglas B. Graham
Operations Manager: Gennaro C. Esposito
Assistant Production Editor: Feliciano Madrid
Quality Control: Robert L. Young (director),
James J. Cox (assistant),
Michael G. Wight (associate)
Art Coordinator: Anne B. Landry
Art Assistant: Susan Kuntz
Copy Staff: Susan B. Galloway (chief),
Cynthia Kleinfeld, Florence Keith,
Celia Beattie
Traffic: Jeanne Potter
Correspondents: Elisabeth Kraemer (Bonn); Margot
Hapgood, Dorothy Bacon (London); Susan Jonas,
Lucy T. Voulgaris (New York); Maria Vincenza
Aloisi, Josephine du Brusle (Paris); Ann Natanson
(Rome). Valuable assistance was also provided by
Carolyn T. Chubet, Miriam Hsia (New York).

The Encyclopedia of Collectibles
was created under the supervision
of Time-Life Books by
TREE COMMUNICATIONS, INC.
President: Rodney Friedman
Publisher: Bruce Michel
Vice President: Ronald Gross
Secretary: Paul Levin

The Encyclopedia of Collectibles
Editor: Andrea DiNoto
Art Director: Sara Burris
Chief Researcher: Cathy Cashion
Assistant Text Editors: Linda Campbell
Franklin, Judson Mead
Photographers: David Arky, Steven Mays
Assistant Art Director: Christopher Jones
Art Assistant: David Nehila
Researchers: Anna-Teresa Callen, Alix Gudefin,
Enid Klass, Margaret Mooney, Dennis Southers
Writers: Sally Clark, Lee Dennis,
William C. Ketchum Jr., Judy Wade, Susan Young
Contributing Editors: Colin Leinster, Pat Murray,
David S. Thomson, Henry Wiencek

Editorial Consultant: Jay Gold
Consultants for this volume: Don Walters (Folk Art);
J. Kenny Halstead (Frogs); Jim Ducote, Gordon
McClelland (Fruit-Crate Labels); Herbert Siegel
(Games); Janet Seagle (Golf Clubs); Sally Hopkins
(Greeting Cards); Robert W. Lowe, Warren Moore
(Guns); Diane Malhmood (Hatpins); Carla
Tscherny (Hats); Joel Kopp, Kate Kopp (Hooked
Rugs); Don Berkebile, Thomas Ryder (Horse-
drawn Carriages)

The Cover: Brilliant colors and striking design make
labels like these—once intended for the ends of
wooden fruit crates—desirable collectibles. Of the
dozen reproduced here, all but three are labels
promoting California citrus, the type sought most
frequently by collectors.

Acknowledgments: Hicks painting, page 11, and
fractur, page 13, courtesy of The Museum of
American Folk Art, New York; Stringfield
sculpture, second from left, page 20, courtesy of
H. R. Bradley Smith; netsukes, page 25, courtesy
of H. B. Altman, Objects of Vertu, New York;
tomato can label, page 38, courtesy of Carol Wald;
syrup can label, page 38, courtesy of Linda
Campbell Franklin; Yves game, page 49, courtesy
of Herbert J. Siegel; Monopoly game, page
54, courtesy of Parker Brothers; golf clubs, page
61, courtesy of Richard E. Bednarek; golf clubs,
pages 64-65, courtesy of the U.S.G.A. Museum,
Far Hills, New Jersey; greeting cards, pages 80-81,
courtesy of Linda Campbell Franklin; powder
horns, page 85, and pair of English pistols, page
91, courtesy of Warren Moore; Boutet flintlock
rifle and pistols and German target rifle, pages 90-
91, courtesy of The Metropolitan Museum of Art,
New York; M1 Carbine and Walther P 38 pistol,
pages 96-97, courtesy of Centre Firearms Co., Inc.,
New York; men's hats, pages 122, 125 and 127,
and hats, pages 124, 128 and 129, courtesy of
Robert Pusilo.

Library of Congress Cataloging in Publication Data
(The encyclopedia of collectibles.)
Includes bibliographies.
1. Americana. 2. Antiques—United States.
I. Time-Life Books.
NK805.E63   745.1'09'0973   77-99201
ISBN 0-8094-2764-8
ISBN 0-8094-2763-X lib. bdg.

Contents

Folk Art
Striking Creations of Native Talent

You might think that all the fine American folk art was by now locked up in museums or dealers' stocks, accessible only to those who build their collections by writing large checks. Yet folk art—paintings and sculptures of artists who have no formal training—still is being created all over America, and recent works can be picked up for a few dollars by anyone perceptive enough to recognize good art when he sees it. Even collectibles from the 19th Century can be discovered.

A schoolteacher in New England went to a flea market, saw a watercolor portrait of a woman and bought it for $6; months later she took advantage of the free appraisal clinic offered sporadically by a large New York City auction gallery and brought the picture in, rolled up in a shopping bag. The clinic appraiser identified it as an early-19th Century painting by the highly regarded husband-and-wife team of S. A. and R. W. Shute. It was auctioned off for $22,000.

One reason such prizes continue to turn up is the relatively recent elevation of American folk art to high sta-

The 19th Century carver of this small painted wooden figure made a visual joke, turning arms and tail coat into feathers of a birdman.

Herbert W. Hemphill Jr. began collecting folk art and writing books and articles about it during the 1950s. He specializes in 20th Century works, a number of which have been loaned to museums.

tus. Until the 1920s it was ignored, for it is unsophisticated, produced by men and women whose native talents have not been refined by academic training or exposure to the masterpieces of the past.

Most folk art is done without regard to realistic size

The artist of the oil portrait at left, done on the wood from a drawer bottom, is unknown, but even so, the picture is valuable for its age and quality. The style of the wig dates the portrait to the late 1700s.

and scale: one subject may be depicted larger than everything else in the work simply to indicate its importance. Perspective—the indication of what is near and what is far away—is sometimes distorted, and forms are stylized. When an artist like Picasso deviates from established practice in that way, he deviates deliberately. The folk artist does so because he does not know or care about the practice.

Deliberate distortions by moderns such as Picasso, who had been influenced by African primitive works, began affecting U.S. artists around World War I and led them to recognize the value of the folk art in their own country. In the 1920s they became collectors.

But much of the popular interest is owed to the encouragement provided by two wealthy women. One was Gertrude Vanderbilt Whitney, daughter of the Commodore and herself a sculptor. The first major exhibit of folk art was held in 1924 at the Whitney Studio Club in New York City, an artists' gathering place that she established and then later expanded into the famous Whitney Museum of American Art. The other aristocratic enthusiast was Abby Aldrich Rockefeller, who helped establish the Museum of Modern Art in New York City and the Colonial Williamsburg restoration in Virginia, where an outstanding collection of folk art is housed in a museum bearing her name.

In museums such as the Whitney and Rockefeller you can see the works of such 18th and 19th Century masters as William Matthew Prior, a Boston-based portrait painter who advertised a "flat likeness without shade or shadow" for $2.17, and Mr. and Mrs. Shute—a Shute portrait of a little girl patting her puppy broke records for prices paid for folk-art watercolors by bringing $42,500 at a 1978 auction.

Although very old works such as these are very valuable, lucky finds like the New England schoolteacher's Shute can still be made. It is much easier to find four special types of folk art quite different from the Hicks and Shute masterpieces: mourning pictures, theorem paintings, calligraphic drawings and fracturs, examples of which appear on pages 12 and 13. The making of mourning and theorem pictures was considered a proper pastime for genteel ladies and was taught in the female academies of the 19th Century. Mourning pictures in ink, watercolors or embroidery were done to commemorate the death of someone prominent or of someone who was close to the artist. They almost always included a weeping willow tree, and usually depicted mourners at a monument that was inscribed with the name of the deceased and the date.

Theorem paintings, popular between 1800 and 1840, were still lifes done with purchased stencils, much like modern painting-by-the-numbers. Many are painted on velvet, silk or wool, and the best incorporate the artists' individual ideas so that they transcend the limitations of the commercial stencils.

Calligraphic drawings had their origin in the elegant handwriting style invented by Platt Rogers Spencer and were imitations of engravings, done in the thick and thin strokes of Spencerian handwriting. They were popular at a time, before the typewriter, when skillful penmanship was a social asset and a prerequisite for aspiring clerks. Many of the drawings were intended to be demonstrations of the artist's professional skill in penmanship rather than works of art, although the one reproduced on page 12 was clearly a personal gift.

Fracturs are illuminated handwritten documents that record births, baptisms and marriages. The name comes from the German typeface on which the lettering was modeled, and the art itself was brought to this country by immigrants from Germany. If you visit areas in which these people have settled—in Pennsylvania, Virginia, North Carolina, Ohio, Indiana and Texas—make it a point to look through Bibles at yard sales. Fracturs were often placed between the pages for safekeeping or made directly on the family-record pages.

Unless you find a fractur in an old German Bible or come across a Shute painting in a flea market, you must expect 19th Century folk art to be costly—a theorem painting went for $600 in a 1978 auction. This is not true of most 20th Century folk art. My particular interest is in contemporary works, and I search them out wherever I go, offering a price for each related to the appeal it has for me.

When I come into a small town, I walk around to look in windows. Sometimes I find something right off— bird carvings in a barbershop, say, or paintings in a bar. (It was in a drugstore that a collector first discovered the paintings of Grandma Moses, probably the most famous

The subject's clothing forms bold patterns in this oil by Ammi Phillips of Connecticut, typical of portraits of the early 19th Century.

folk artist of this century.) I also ask people like the ministers and the editor of the newspaper if they know of any artists doing work like ones I show them in a book I carry with me. Country stores are good places to look. Arts-and-crafts fairs, church bazaars and even yard sales should not be overlooked. And it is worth bearing in mind that valuable folk carvings have been found in communities near old lumber camps in Michigan, where the lumbermen have traditionally whiled away winter evenings whittling.

The market in folk art is lively. Value depends on esthetic judgments, and few experts agree on what constitutes beauty in art. The best advice is: buy what you like. Only by pleasing yourself can you give your collection its own spirit. That spirit is definitely in a portrait that a Southern folk artist is doing of me right now. It has everything I am attracted to in folk art: vivid coloring, stylized form and characterization. It even has unorthodox scale: it is 7 feet tall and 4 feet wide.

For related material, see the article on Hooked Rugs in this volume, and on Carousel Animals, Chalkware, Coverlets, Decoys, Nautical Gear, Quilts, Redware, Samplers, Silhouettes, Stoneware, Tramp Art and Weather Vanes in separate volumes of this encyclopedia.

An oil painting by an unknown artist done around 1840 depicts a woman and flowers in glowing colors. It is unusual because, unlike most portraits, it is almost square, 30 by 32 inches.

Emily Eastman based this watercolor on prints popular around 1820. All her works show similar facial expressions.

An 1860 watercolor by Mrs. S. G. Armstrong copies a lithograph by Nathaniel Currier of the Currier & Ives firm.

An unsigned oil painted around 1850 and entitled "Echo Rock" is remarkable for its composition and draftmanship. The snowy path dividing the 36-by-29-inch scene in half commands attention, and drama is heightened by the stag's muscularity. Although most of the painting is in scale, the two horses' heads at lower right are unrealistically small.

Edward Hicks did numerous versions of "The Peaceable Kingdom" (right) as well as many other paintings. The allegory combines history—William Penn is shown with Indians (far left)—and religion. Hicks fervently believed that in America the prophecy of Isaiah—that the wolf and the lamb shall lie down together—would come true.

The still life at right was painted with paper stencils for each fruit and leaf. Such 19th Century pictures, called theorems because they were done to formula, were often used as gifts. A complex and many-colored theorem like this is rarely found in perfect condition.

Calligraphic drawings using penmanship skills, like this long—19 inches—image of the huntress Diana riding a deer, were often made as gifts by young men preparing for clerkships. The flourishes at lower left nearly conceal the words "Your Dear Friend Kyse."

The birth and baptism of Johan Martin Eijer in 1795, probably in Pennsylvania, is announced in an elaborately embellished certificate called a fractur. This type of folk art, which was brought to the United States by German immigrants, was frequently done by a minister or schoolmaster.

The death of George Washington in 1799 set off a vogue for mourning pictures following a more-or-less standard format, and for decades afterward similar ones were made to commemorate the loss of a family member. This 1805 watercolor is unusual for the gold on the angel's wings and the pinpricking of the leaves of the bushes at left—a touch that gives texture and creates the look of embroidery.

Echoing the drooping willow in the picture on page 13, this unusual carving was one of several wooden roof ornaments, 16 inches tall, made for a hearse about 1870.

A carved-wood penguin, 20 inches high, betrays the weathering it received standing for many decades on a gatepost at a Nantucket Island yacht club. It was made in the 1880s.

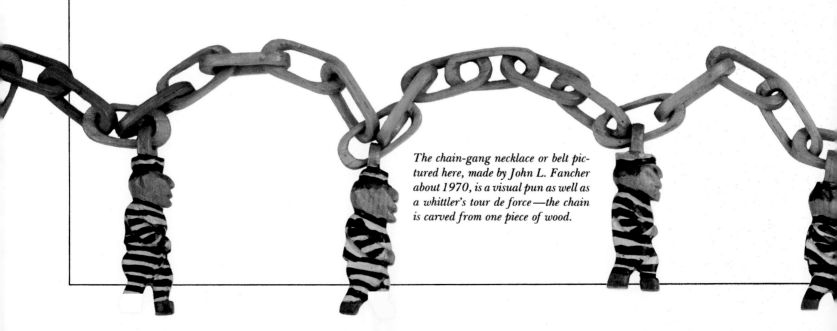

The chain-gang necklace or belt pictured here, made by John L. Fancher about 1970, is a visual pun as well as a whittler's tour de force—the chain is carved from one piece of wood.

Sculptured Fancies for Ornament

Many folk-art collectors make practically no distinction between sculpture created for art's sake—like the works on page 7 and pages 18 to 21—and three-dimensional objects that, like the ones shown here, are more or less useful. Some embellish utilitarian necessities, such as the penguin gatepost finial at left and the willow hearse ornament at far left. Others seem inspired by a practical purpose—as if the artist employed the useful aspect of his creation to make a joke. The bandbox at right would not be so humorous if it were not also a box for old-fashioned detachable collars, or collar bands.

A bandstand with a full quota of musicians has a roof that lifts off to reveal space for collar bands, the detachable shirt collars worn by men into the 1920s.

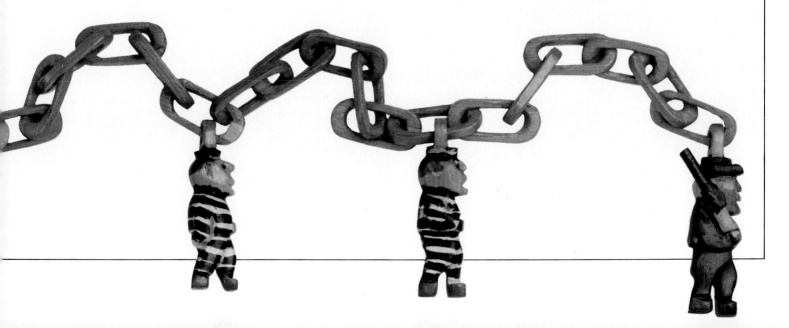

The painting above, "Waterfront at Night, Spectacular Night," and its frame were made in 1964 by Alex Maldonado of San Francisco. The style of his depiction of the city's harbor makes it easy to see why Maldonado also enjoys doing pictures illustrating themes of science fiction.

WATERFRONT
"SPECTACULAR NIGHT"
ALEX MALDONADO
8-5-6?

A tiger moving into mysterious space was painted by Martin Ramirez; mute most of his life, he died in an institution in 1960.

"Coaltown U.S.A." was painted on hardboard by Jack Savitsky, a jobless miner who turned to art when he was past 50.

Victor Joseph Gatto, onetime plumber's helper—among other things—painted his vision of Paradise before his death in 1965.

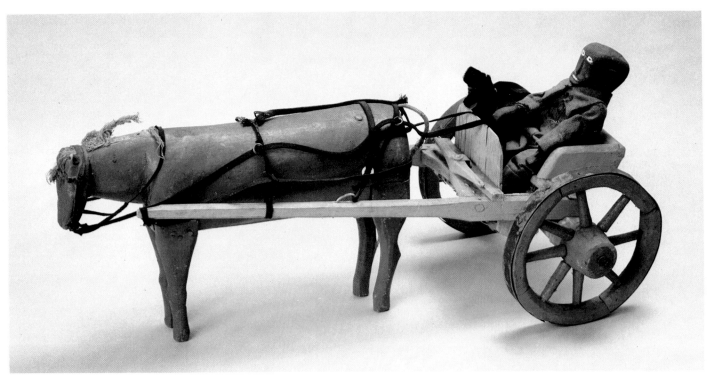

A 2-foot-long articulated sculpture by W. S. Rosenbaum was made of jointed pieces of wood. It dates from the 1920s and depicts a black mailman driving a horse-drawn cart. Scenes of everyday life like this one are called genre sculpture; they were not made as toys.

This grim genre sculpture, only 11 inches long, depicts a sow trying to kill the runt of a litter. The crank in the sow's flank is attached to a wire that causes the runt to move as if the sow were shaking it to death. The farmer holds a stick to poke the sow and make it drop the runt.

A gorilla was made by Felipe Archuleta, a New Mexico carpenter. The carving, covered with a mixture of sawdust and glue and then painted, stands 40 inches high.

The creator of the gorilla above also made this whimsical snake, 6 ½ feet long, its body assembled from bottle caps and given a carved and painted head and tail. Friends collect bottle caps for Archuleta to make into sculpture.

The American tradition of whittling wood with a pocketknife is carried on by many 20th Century folk artists, such as West Virginian S. L. Jones, who made these country musicians, each a little more than 2 feet tall.

Four wooden beauties, each nearly 2 feet tall, were made in the 1960s and 1970s by Clarence Stringfield of Erin, Tennessee. A onetime cabinetry teacher, he repaired gunstocks and played a fiddle that he carved himself.

A farmer in neatly pressed overalls, almost a foot tall, is the work of Kentucky mountaineer Edgar Tolson, who once whittled false teeth.

MUSEUMS

Abby Aldrich Rockefeller Folk Art Collection
Williamsburg, Virginia 23185

Greenfield Village and Henry Ford Museum
Dearborn, Michigan 48121

Museum of American Folk Art
New York, New York 10019

Museum of International Folk Art
Santa Fe, New Mexico 87501

Old Sturbridge Village
Sturbridge, Massachusetts 01566

Philadelphia Museum of Art
Philadelphia, Pennsylvania 19101

Shelburne Museum
Shelburne, Vermont 05482

PERIODICALS

The Clarion—America's Folk Art Magazine, Museum of American Folk Art, New York, New York 10019

BOOKS

Ames, Kenneth L., *Beyond Necessity: Art in the Folk Tradition.* The Winterthur Museum, 1977.

Bishop, Robert, *American Folk Sculpture.* E. P. Dutton & Co., Inc., 1974.

Black, Mary, and Jean Lipman, *American Folk Painting.* Clarkson N. Potter, Inc., 1966.

Folk Art in America: A Living Tradition. The High Museum of Art, 1974.

Hemphill, Herbert W., Jr., ed., *Folk Sculpture USA.* The Brooklyn Museum, 1976.

Hemphill, Herbert W., Jr., and Julia Weissman, *Twentieth-Century American Folk Art and Artists.* E. P. Dutton & Co., Inc., 1974.

Hornung, Clarence P., *Treasury of American Design,* 2 vols. Harry N. Abrams, Inc., 1972.

Lipman, Jean:
American Folk Art in Wood, Metal and Stone. Dover Publications, Inc., 1972.
American Primitive Painting. Dover Publications, Inc., 1969.

Lipman, Jean, and Alice Winchester, *The Flowering of American Folk Art: 1776-1876.* The Viking Press, 1974.

Shelley, Donald A., *The Fraktur-Writings or Illuminated Manuscripts of the Pennsylvania Germans.* The Pennsylvania German Folklore Society, 1961.

Frogs
Amphibians with Bug-eyed Charm

Some people who go abroad weigh themselves down with phrase books. But when I travel, I need only a single word, appropriately translated: *żaba,* when a business trip takes me to Poland; *rana* for a Spanish vacation; *béka* in Hungary; and syllables that sound like *dofdaah* when I go to the Middle East. They all mean the same thing—frog. I have been collecting frog figurines since the age of six when my sister, shivery with the knowledge of what I was catching in the ponds near our home, presented me with a frog made of lead. Today that weighty amphibian is the dean of my collection of approximately 800 frogs and their warty-skinned cousins, the toads.

Discovering the wonder of these creatures has not been mine alone. Collecting frogs is a surprisingly com-

---

Larry Prus has collected frog figures since early childhood, which he spent in a rural area with ponds where frogs abounded. He is the proprietor of a commercial art studio.

---

petitive hobby; miniatures in bronze have fetched prices of more than $100 in the 1970s. Nor is interest in them new. In ancient Greece, for example, children often wore toad amulets fashioned from terra cotta, and in Japan the frog and the toad have for three centuries been popular motifs for netsuke, the miniature carved-ivory decorations used on accessories such as purses and tobacco pouches.

Among the names that frog collectors search out today are Zsolnay, Bergman and Staffordshire. The Zsolnay pottery of Pécs, Hungary, was founded in 1862. After years of experimentation, the Zsolnay potters began turning out fine porcelain that had intense color and a gleaming, iridescent glaze. All Zsolnay ceramics, not only the frogs, are much in demand—and easily identified: "Zsolnay Pécs" is stamped on the base of every piece, along with a picture of Pécs Cathedral. The factory still operates, and 20th Century work bears the additional word "Hungary."

Another enterprise launched in the 19th Century, the Bergman foundry was one of several in Vienna that created a great variety of painted bronze animals, among them frogs highly valued by many collectors. Bergman frogs, often comically attired, borrow human attributes:

they play musical instruments, ride seesaws and even relax in rocking chairs. The company, whose 19th Century pieces are considered highly valuable because of the quality of their hand decoration, was in business just short of a century; it began operation in 1855 and closed its doors in 1954.

Contemporaneously with Bergman and Zsolnay, the potters of Staffordshire, England, were making pint and pint-and-a-half frog mugs, named for the molded clay beasts that lurk in their bottoms. As pub regulars would tell strangers, a barkeep could serve ale or beer in one of these mugs to a tipsy customer and hope that a face-to-face confrontation with a popeyed, reproachful frog countenance would send the toper home.

A majority of frog mugs are made of white earthenware, and they are often decorated on the outside with hand-painted village drinking scenes. Depending on their condition, individual 19th Century frog mugs sold in the 1970s for around $250; 20th Century mugs, more crudely made, were less expensive.

My own collection also includes many American-made frogs such as a group of musicians on a clock, paperweights and a tin frog jauntily riding a tricycle. Perhaps the most unusual of these native products is the sewer-pipe sculpture shown on page 29. Workers in clay-pipe factories in the 19th and early 20th Centuries often whiled away spare time by molding whimsical animal figures out of the clay and firing them in the company kilns along with the sewer pipe. Only rarely did they sculpt frogs, however, and in the late 1970s a collector paid $150 for one.

Good sources for sewer-pipe sculptures—and also for frogs or toads carved from semiprecious stones such as bloodstone, jade or malachite—are auctions that advertise *objets de vertu* (objects of a curious and antique nature). Keeping your eyes peeled when you travel is essential, of course. And once word of your hobby has spread, people will know what to give you for a present. Recently, Italian friends sent me five Venetian glass frogs—*granocchia* in Italian—with a short and, to me, not unflattering note: "These remind us of you."

A frog "prince" wears the high-luster glaze that identifies it as a Zsolnay pottery product. This porcelain piece, from about 1900, is 3 inches high.

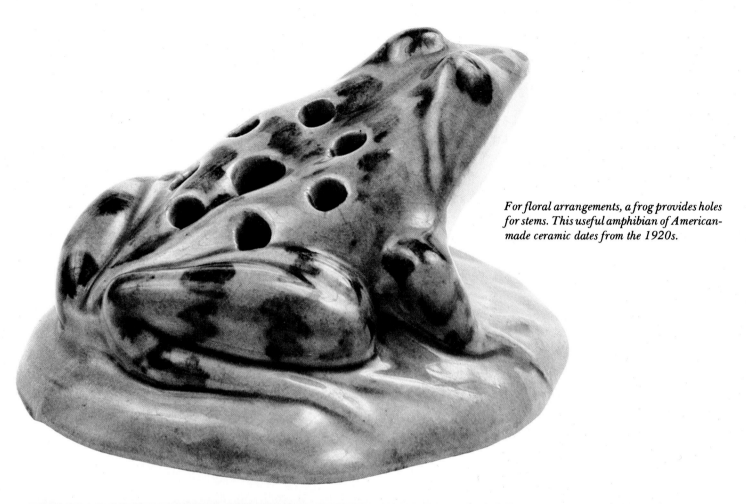

For floral arrangements, a frog provides holes for stems. This useful amphibian of American-made ceramic dates from the 1920s.

Finely crafted frogs decorate these two paperweights. At left, the glazed ceramic figure is molded in one piece with an unglazed base, and dates *from about 1890; it was made in the U.S. The other, with a porphyry base, is British, made of bronze about 1920.*

At left and above are Japanese ivory netsukes, or toggles, made to be worn with kimonos. They are 2 inches high, with eyes of inlaid jet. Antique netsukes command thousands of dollars. These contemporary examples—a pair of toads and the mythological toad-toting hermit Gama Sennin—are valued in the hundreds of dollars.

Admonitory frogs glare from the bottoms of these 19th Century English earthenware mugs, signaling "last drink" to overindulgent beer- and ale bibbers. The mug at left bears an original painting, the other two have molded and hand-tinted relief decoration.

On a foot-high bronze-sheathed clock made in 1885 by Chicago's Golden Novelty Company, an ebullient baton-wielding frog-conductor leads a duet for flute and banjo as an audience of one frog listens. The clock's face in this unique piece is the body of the banjo.

Place a coin on the small frog, trip a lever, and the coin is kicked into the larger frog's mouth. This cast-iron bank was made in 1882.

This frog, made of wood in Germany about 1860, functions as an overnight pocket-watch holder. It opens up to accommodate the watch.

A functional frog, dating from the 1860s, does duty as a paper embosser. The stamp reads "Bradbury & Sweat," a Maine law firm.

Wind it up, and a nattily dressed frog will pedal its tricycle. Made in the 1890s, this tin toy is valued primarily because of its age.

The Bergman foundry of Vienna made this pair of bronze frogs after 1850. The unusual size of the piece —almost a foot long —increases its value.

Drummer, violinist and flutist, each only 2 inches high, form a typical Bergman-foundry trio, cast before World War I. The drum props up the percussionist, while unobtrusive supports, painted to suggest grassy earth, hold the other instrumentalists erect.

The figure at right is a sewer-pipe sculpture; it was made around 1870 by a worker amusing himself in an Ohio pipe factory.

The frogs above and at right are made of bloodstone, a quartzlike rock with red flecks. German in origin, they date from the late 19th Century.

BOOKS

Boger, Louise Ade, *The Dictionary of World Pottery and Porcelain.* Charles Scribner's Sons, 1971.

Fruit-Crate Labels
Glowing Promises of Goodness

This deliberately plain label identified fruit inferior in appearance but good inside.

When my father migrated from Illinois, by way of the Dakota territory, to farm in California in 1892, that state's image was being established by the labels identifying crates of oranges, lemons, grapes and other fruits grown in its hospitable climate. The labels suggested a paradise of bountiful yields in a lush land where the earth was fertile, the women beautiful, the men sturdy and the children healthy.

Now those fruit-crate labels evoke an era that is long gone by. For the California of today has less room than it previously had for citrus groves like the one my father started. Between 1940 and the early 1950s the population of the state almost doubled. Groves were uprooted and packing houses were torn down to make way for suburbs and shopping malls. And the glowing lithographed labels were phased out, as cardboard boxes, which were ink-stamped with identification, were introduced to replace the expensive wooden fruit crates. It was during this period, the early 1950s, that collecting fruit-crate labels actually got under way.

I did not become interested in collecting until some years later when, working as director of a citrus-packing

---

Ray Soper, a retired lemon grower who planted his first trees in 1931 in San Bernardino, California, comes from a family of citrus farmers.

---

house, I realized the historical value of the old labels. I began to collect some from local packing houses still in operation. Then one day a field superintendent told me about an old chicken house that was filled with thousands of labels pasted onto "heads" (the ends of the old wooden packing crates).

When I visited the chicken house I found a stack of heads that must have measured 15 feet long, 8 feet wide and 7 feet high. It was obvious that the pile was destined to become firewood in a potbellied stove that was standing nearby. I trucked the crate ends home and began the slow process of soaking the labels free from the

wood. It was then that I knew I had become a collector.

Some of the old fruit-crate labels are so plentiful they can be bought for less than a dollar apiece from mail-order label dealers who sell unused specimens that have been discovered in warehouses and packing houses. These dealers advertise in magazines such as *Antiques Trader* and will send out mimeographed catalogues of their inventory upon request. But some of the labels are quite scarce. Among those featuring pictures of animals, for example, the Fearless orange label that is reproduced on page 33 is a valuable find.

Rarity is not the only criterion of a label's value. Design also is important. Labels from orange crates, for some reason, were more imaginatively designed than those from other fruit crates, and are therefore worth more. The California labels as a group are worth more than those from Florida or other fruit-producing states, mainly because Californians are the most avid collectors and have already picked up most of the local labels.

Age is another factor. The oldest—and rarest—labels date back to the 1880s. It was then that growers in southern California, faced with stiff competition from foreign fruitgrowers, sought to promote their produce by using colorful labels; they turned to San Francisco lithographers, who had already achieved local fame with the ornate stock certificates they had made following the gold rush. None of the San Francisco lithographers is as important to collectors as the company operated by Max Schmidt, a young German immigrant who had won local recognition by producing labels for wine bottles.

Working with salesman-artist teams—called scissor men because they could make up label designs on the spot from sketches and cutouts from stock designs—Schmidt traveled through such towns as Riverside, Pasadena and Santa Ana looking for customers. Because of

Golden sunbeams bathe the earth on a label dating from around 1900. A specimen like this one sold in 1978 for $85.

F. B. Devine

SUNBEAM

F B

BRAND

Oranges

Lemons

GROWN AND PACKED IN

RIVERSIDE
Riverside County
CALIF.

CALIFORNIA.

REGISTERED

this stock system, the same designs were used by different growers: the La Loma Queen *(page 39)*, for example, turns up with several different brand names, as does the California Slab Apricots *(pages 36-37)*.

In 1898, Schmidt allied himself with the label departments of other lithography houses to form the Mutual Litho Company. Mutual played a big role in early label production up to the time of the San Francisco earthquake of 1906, when its plant was destroyed. Today, Mutual labels—identifiable by the company name printed in the lower left-hand corner—are among the rarest a collector can find.

In addition to lithographers' names, certain designs give a clue to the age of a label. In 1907, the California Fruit Growers Exchange decided to identify its top-grade fruit with the Sunkist seal—an orange inside a sunburst *(page 44)*. This design was used on labels until 1917 when it was replaced by a seal showing an orange wrapped in tissue *(page 33)*. The overall style of the design also helps date labels. Those made from the 1880s to the late 1920s had highly detailed, picturesque scenes with a three-dimensional effect. Labels of this style and age are not easy to come by, and prices are high—the Airship label, made around 1910 *(page 45)*, brought an offer of $125 in 1978.

In the 1920s, advertising art became bolder, simpler and flatter, much like poster art. You can see the difference by comparing the 1910 Airship with the 1940s Palomar on page 40.

Some collectors look for labels that have been updated three or four times. The Athlete labels on page 42 (under which many of my own lemons were shipped) reveal changes in art and clothing styles that took place over 10 years. On another updated label the California landscape changes over the decades: a Silver Moon label from around 1900 depicts a mission in California that is surrounded by orange groves; in a 1920s version, a few lights from houses appear on the horizon; and, in the final version, from the 1940s, suburban Los Angeles surrounds the mission.

Good buys in labels sometimes turn up in places far from the prime sources in California. In 1974 an old mom-and-pop grocery store in Wisconsin advertised that it had 30 old fruit crates for sale. I took the bait and had the crate heads sent to me. I soaked the labels off—some gave me trouble, coming off in pieces. I dried these scraps and pasted them onto thin backing paper. The work was worth the trouble: all of the labels were valuable and a few, like the Grizzly Giant and Half Moon, were rare.

The Chinese lettering across the top of this label for California grapes, which dates from the late 1940s, suggests that the packer had buyers for San Francisco's and New York City's Chinatowns in mind.

This Angora orange-crate label, which was issued in 1925, is one of many that used animals, cuddly or fearsome, as their subject. Another, presumably also aimed at cat lovers, was Tomcat.

The seal of an orange wrapped in tissue paper indicates that Strength was marketed by the California Fruit Growers Exchange, that the fruit was top quality—Sunkist—and that it came on the market after 1917.

When the Fearless packing house went out of business in the 1950s, unused labels were discarded and few examples survive. The Silver Seal was the distributor's quality symbol, like rival Sunkist's orange.

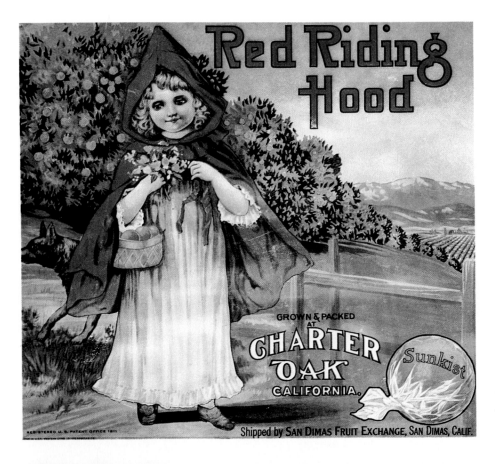

A series of Red Riding Hood labels was made from 1911 to the 1930s. In the version at left, used in the 1920s, Red Riding Hood carries a basket of oranges to Grandma's house.

The John Alden label at left, like the Red Riding Hood example above, is one of a series. Complete sets, showing the variations over the years, are particularly desirable.

Some collectors specialize in labels that show flowers, making prices high for this category. The Wildflower label above is a rare one that was printed around 1900. It sold for $40 in 1978. A Shasta Daisy, which is even rarer, has fetched $100.

This Orange Blossom label was made in the 1890s for Arthur Gregory, the grower who founded one of the large distribution cooperatives.

The Union Club label was produced in San Francisco by H. S. Crocker, one of the city's outstanding lithographers.

CALIFO
SLAB AI

PREPARED WITH
SULPHUR DIOXIDE

Packed By RICHMOND-CHASE CO

This label was used by more than one producer of apricots but it identified dried rather than fresh fruit. The box contained a slab, 40 pounds of apricots that

ORNIA
RICOTS

25 LBS. NET WEIGHT

SAN JOSE, CALIFORNIA

Idealized Pictures from Cans and Boxes

The tomato-can label above is valued because the copyright date — 1904 — is printed at the bottom, because the colors are vivid and *the printing in general is of high quality, and because the photo-graph of the little girl is appealing.*

This label for a can of sugar-cane syrup from Georgia is desirable because of its complicated design and the embossed, or raised, printing.

Many kinds of labels for food containers, in addition to those for fruit crates, are sought by collectors. The earliest go back to about the 1820s. These were printed for or by the communal societies known as Shakers for the jars and boxes in which they sold herbs, preserves, extracts, ointments and seeds. These simple, rectangular labels bore only the name of the product within and of the Shaker group that produced it. Because the labels were hand-cut with scissors from large printed sheets, their edges often are not straight. Huge quantities were printed—in 1870 alone more than a million of these labels were used on containers for herbs and extracts—but in spite of the numbers they are fairly rare

and quite desirable today, particularly the oldest ones.

Labels for commercially produced food containers are also highly collectible. Various parts of the country had specialties that a collector can look for, and many collectors limit themselves to a type of food or a region. For example, Baltimore, a packing and shipping center from the 1870s on, specialized in peaches and oysters. Cane syrup, peanut butter and pickles came from Georgia.

All types of labels—including many for products other than food, such as sewing needles and medicines—are available at the large paper shows that are held annually in different parts of the country, and through label dealers and advertisements in periodicals.

The idealized señorita decorating the La Loma Queen orange label above also lent her charm to Lady Barbara, Wheeler's Choice and Spanish Girl brands, all of which used the same design.

A svelte diver is one of many depictions of the female form that added modest sex appeal to labels. She adorns an apple label of the 1920s, when California produced about a third as many apples as oranges.

This label, made in 1915, is unusual because its picture—an attractive homemaker proudly displaying a pie prepared from

Appeal lemons—is one of the few in which a dish cooked from the fruit is used to make a selling point.

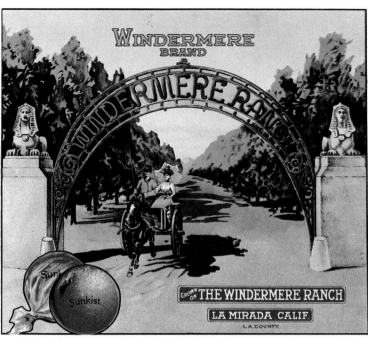

The style of the Sunkist seal indicates this Windermere label was made after World War I, but the lavish California ranch scene has a turn-of-the-century look. Researchers found that an old design had been reused in the 1920s.

California landmarks are a popular collecting specialty. The style of the automobile pictured above indicates that the Palomar label was made about the same time the famous observatory was opened, in 1948.

An idealized Pacific beach scene, amply supplied with bathing beauties, decorates this rare label. Only three copies are known to survive.

LEMONS

SIDE
BRAND

CALIFORNIA
Red Ball

GROWN IN U. S. A.

Battle Front

BRAND

SUNFLOWER PACKING CORPORATION
PORTERVILLE, CALIFORNIA

The Battle Front label was used during World War II, when much fruit went to the armed forces. It was preceded in World War I and the Spanish-American War by the Over There and Volunteer labels among others. Wartime labels are a collecting specialty of their own.

The two Athlete labels at left are an example of updating. The lone cross-country runner in the 1920s version at top has been replaced at bottom by three sprinters in a 1930s stadium scene—perhaps the Los Angeles Olympics of 1932. The word brogdex refers to a process used to preserve citrus fruit.

An Indian belle and her lover tryst in a grapefruit grove (left) on a label made in 1910. Foothill meant the fruit came from orchards on ground slightly higher than average; at this elevation the air was moister and the fruit therefore sweeter.

In a 1940s label a cowboy ropes an orange. Other labels with Western themes depict scouts, gold miners and such famous figures as Buffalo Bill.

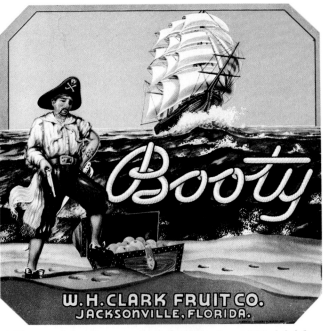

A pirate guards a treasure chest of oranges in a 1940s label from Florida. Because it does not come from California, its value suffers.

This Airship citrus label goes back to around 1910. Only four copies like it are known to exist; the 1978 price for the label above was $200. In later, updated versions label makers replaced the pedaling pilot and his airship first with a biplane and then with a four-engined airliner.

LIBRARIES
Huntington Library
San Marino, California 91108

Pomona Public Library
Pomona, California 91766

Shields Library, University of California
Davis, California 95616

COLLECTORS ORGANIZATIONS
Tri-County Citrus Label Collectors
P.O. Box 187
Riverside, California 92502

Pacific Antique Labels Society
P.O. Box 2552
San Bernardino, California 92406

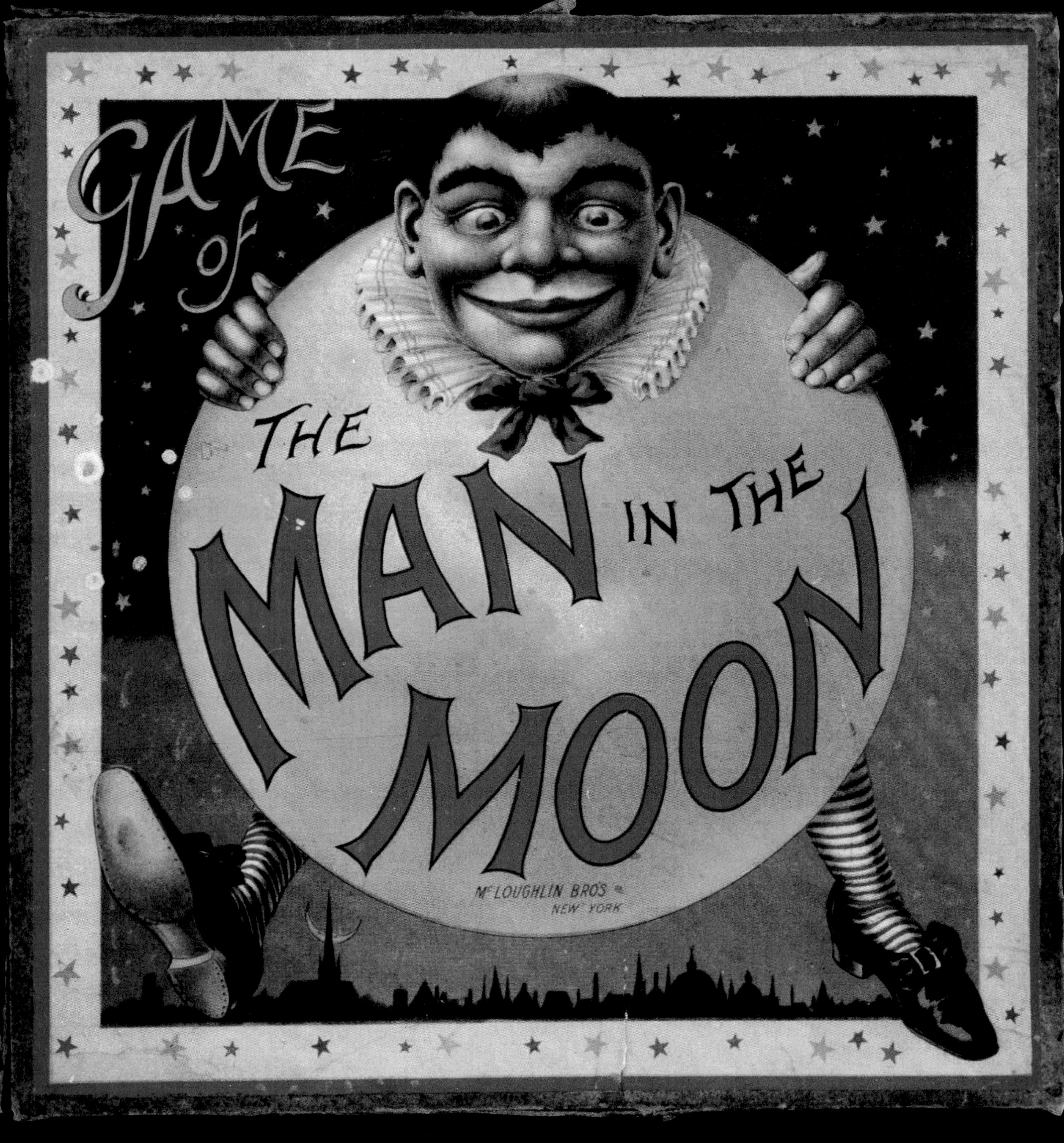
GAME of
THE
MAN IN THE
MOON
MC LOUGHLIN BRO'S
NEW YORK

Games
Bright Art of Parlor Amusements

I became a collector by accident, a circumstance I consider absolutely appropriate for a collectible in which chance determines the action. It was my husband's love of poker that got me started. Because of that we bought an antique gaming table at an auction. When we got it home I found two old games in one of the drawers: Minoru, an English game about horse racing, and Wonders of the Deep, a board game of German origin with four small leaden men in diving helmets. I was so taken by their visual appeal that I started looking for others in secondhand shops and flea markets. That was more than 20 years and 700 board games ago.

The kind of game that I collect originated in Italy sometime in the late 1500s with a diversion simply called Goose. Popular all over Europe by the early 1600s, and

Lee Dennis is a freelance writer who started a collection of board games in the mid-1950s. Her acquisitions became so numerous that she converted part of her house into a museum called The Game Preserve.

depending for its progress and outcome on luck rather than skill, the game followed a scheme that has become very familiar: it was a race between players, each moving a piece along a track composed of sections. The object was to get to the end of the track—the goal—first. Some of the sections had instructions that sent a player ahead or back when he landed on them after observing the throw of dice or the action of a spinner.

The name Goose came from the depiction of the bird on certain sections that allowed a player to take a free throw, though no one has explained how a barnyard fowl came to symbolize a second chance. Goose game boards had 63 sections, which were usually illustrated: sometimes scenes of vice appeared on sections that turned a player back, perhaps showing a sleeping man who exemplified sloth or an inebriate waving a bottle; virtue, gracing sections that nudged a player forward, might be represented by two men shaking hands in a demonstration of civility.

As a collector my main interest today is less in the

Bold coloring and stylized art work in this 1901 game are hallmarks of McLoughlin Brothers, Inc., of New York. Many collectors consider McLoughlin games the most beautiful ever produced in America.

games themselves than in the art work of the game boards and their box covers—specifically that of 19th Century American games. Illustrated board games are very much of their time when they are introduced, and they seldom survive their period. It is this transience that makes them appealing to a collector: their special kind of art offers amusing or nostalgic insight into the activities, attitudes and mores of the past.

Cases in point are two games focused on the telegraph as a means of communication (pages 50-51). In the 1880s, when these games appeared, the telegraph company was a familiar and respected part of American life; it was an article of patriotic faith to cheer on the ambitious young fellows depicted on the boxes as they strove, in the game's competitive action, to rise from their humble messenger jobs to become president of the company. In 1901, when the Man in the Moon game appeared (left), no one actually thought in terms of going to the moon, except perhaps early science-fantasy storytellers like the French writer Jules Verne. The title of the game referred to a forgotten child's contest in which the loser became odd man out, or "the man in the moon."

The first American board games were produced by the W. & S. B. Ives Company, a Salem, Massachusetts, printing concern. In 1843, Ives issued Mansion of Happiness, in which the different squares variously penalize sin and repay righteousness. Inspired by Goose, it is the ancestor of every American board game invented since, including the famous Monopoly (page 54). Ives's early games were printed on cardboard and hand-colored by women working assembly-line style, each filling in one color. Mid-19th Century hand-colored games like Mansion of Happiness are very rare, and in 1978 brought more than $150 if in original condition.

The multicolored boards and boxes produced during the second half of the 19th Century and the first few decades of the 20th Century were printed by the process of lithography, and are highly valued by collectors for their vivid colors. Of all the lithographed games, the most valued are those produced by McLoughlin Brothers, Inc., a New York company that issued games, produced toys and published children's books from the 1850s until it was absorbed by Milton Bradley Co. in 1920. In 1978 collectors paid an average of $45 to $50

The Mansion of Happiness was invented by a clergyman's daughter; its goal is the reward of virtue in a sort of para- *dise. The first board game commercially made in America, now very rare, it appeared 20 years before the Civil War.*

for McLoughlin-made games, a tidy markup from their original price of $1 to $1.50.

The search for board games worth collecting follows generally well-worn paths—including the familiar flea markets, charity thrift shops and garage sales. In antique shops, you should visit the toy section, which is where games usually show up. Wherever you search, never underestimate the part played by happenstance in the fortunes of an alert collector. I found my Mansion of Happiness in a box of a dozen games that a secondhand-housewares dealer was about to discard when I walked into his store.

When you examine any game you are thinking of buying, check to see whether it is complete with all its pieces, its spinner or dice, and the directions for play—valuable in themselves and essential if you want to try playing the game. You also should consider the condition of the cover or box. Nothing saddens me more than to see a McLoughlin game with a tag-sale price sticker on its cover because I know that the sticker probably cannot be removed without tearing the paper.

Fortunately, old-fashioned dirt is not a serious prob-

lem. I use hand soap and warm water on newly acquired games and have recovered some of my favorites from oblivion by that simple method. The New Game of Hunting *(page 56)* had only "Hunting" showing through layers of dust and grime on the box when I found it in a secondhand store. I was delighted when careful cleaning revealed a colorful sunset and a cherubic hunter lithographed in the best McLoughlin tradition.

Board games are as popular today as they ever were. New ones continually appear, mirroring contemporary fads and preoccupations; sooner or later they will be considered collectible. Meanwhile, enough survive of the vividly printed games from the past to provide splendid opportunities for collectors of diverse tastes. For many of us there is something quite irresistible about these old parlor amusements that—through the cheerfully bold colors of their boxes and boards—illuminate the outlook of an increasingly remote era in informal and lighthearted guise.

For related material, see the article on Playing Cards in a separate volume of this encyclopedia.

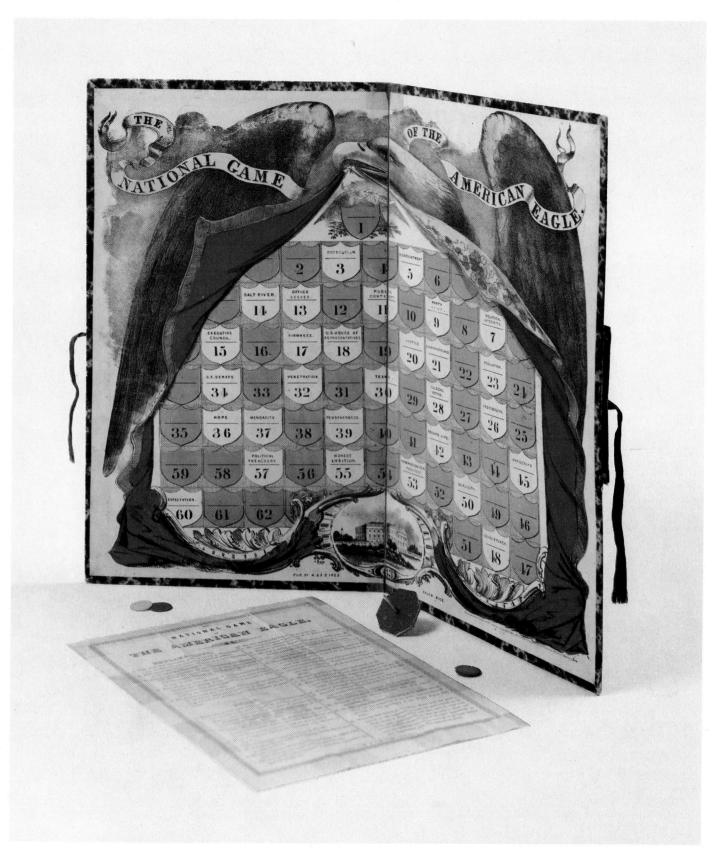

An 1844 game by W. & S. B. Ives, shown above in the only known copy, is based on a campaign for the U.S. Presidency. To win, a player must beat his opponent to the space numbered 63 (the White House), staying out of political hot water wherever possible.

Hard work and hustle pay off in an 1886 McLoughlin game reflecting late-19th Century views on success. Players began as messengers, vying for the top job in the telegraph company.

McLoughlin Brothers borrowed from itself in 1888 when it issued Telegraph Boy, much like its District Messenger Boy game (left). Telegraph Boy is the more valuable collectible because it was issued for only a few years; District Messenger Boy sold for many years.

TRAIN for BOSTON

Parker Brothers
Salem, Mass., U.S.A.

COPYRIGHTED 1900.

Transportation, the motif of these two games, is a natural subject for a contest based on moves across a board. The Parker Brothers game above dates to 1900, when railroading was approaching its zenith in the U.S.

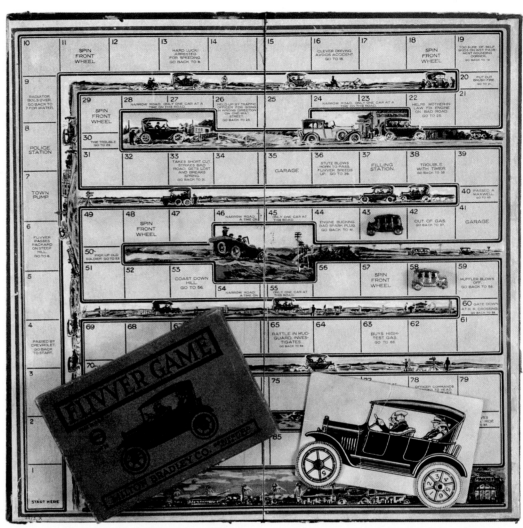

Taking its name from the 1920s slang word for an inexpensive car, the Milton Bradley Flivver Game was an automobile competition that used the spinnable tires of the car on the board as counters.

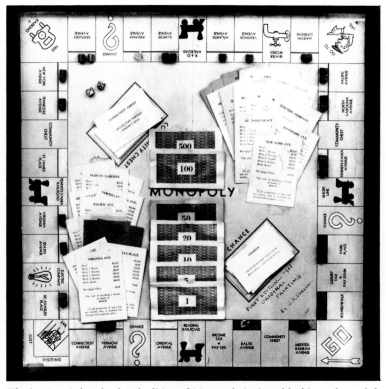

The inventor's hand-colored edition of Monopoly is signed by him at lower left.

The Real Estate Game

A game that has sold more than 80 million copies (a record for board games) might seem to be an unlikely candidate for collectibility. However, the very first edition of Monopoly, which introduced what may be the most famous board-game move—COLLECT $200.00 SALARY AS YOU PASS GO—would certainly be collectible if you could find one for sale. Copies of the first printed edition *(above),* hand-colored by the inventor, an unemployed engineer named Charles Darrow, are extremely scarce. A copy of the first large-scale edition, which was issued by Parker Brothers in 1935, brought a price of $20 in 1978.

Monopoly was originally rejected by Parker Brothers when Darrow offered it in 1934. Among the 52 reasons given to Darrow by Parker Brothers for its lack of interest: the game took too long to play; the company founder, George S. Parker, believed a game that took longer than 45 minutes would bore the players. Darrow's success in selling his own edition of the game at a department store in Philadelphia caused Parker to reconsider. The company then brought out a version of Monopoly very similar to Darrow's original, only to halt production after a year of phenomenal success because Parker felt certain that the game's

popularity would be short-lived. He was of course wrong.

The origin of the game is controversial. According to Parker Brothers, the game was inspired by the Depression. Darrow, an engineer reduced to doing odd jobs, sat down one day and sketched out a game of high finance that recalled happier days spent vacationing in Atlantic City, where the game's real estate operations take place.

But according to others, Monopoly is an adaptation of a game devised in 1904 by Lizzie Magie, called The Landlord's Game. She made it up with the idea of expounding the economic theories of Henry George (1839-1897), an economic reformer who believed that no one should profit from the ownership of property. Magie's theory in inventing the game may have been that the cutthroat nature of its transactions would demonstrate the evils of real estate dealings. The game was spread around the country on hand-made boards by Henry George zealots, who played it with local street names. Darrow, observing the game's success, conceived the idea of making it a commercial venture.

Henry George might well have been appalled had he known of the profits the game brought to Charles Darrow. He retired at 46 on his royalties and spent the rest of his life as a world traveler, gentleman-farmer and orchid collector.

The object of the 1895 McLoughlin Brothers game Hide and Seek was to find out which of the four built-in cups contained a hidden hat and then to carry it home without being captured. Because the board is unusually elaborate, the game is avidly sought after by collectors.

An unlikely trio of golfers on the box cover of an 1896 game makes way for the more serious-looking players pictured on the game board itself (right).

A 1904 game from McLoughlin had cardboard animals, representing hunters' quarry, that were stood up in slots on the board.

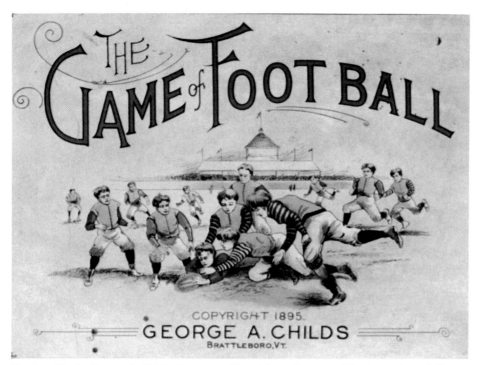

Produced by the George A. Childs Company of Brattleboro, Vermont, The Game of Football came out in 1895 —when college football was still played without helmets.

Milton Bradley's Auto Race Game came with a spinner for each player. Like most Bradley games, Auto Race is undated.

A Genteel Diversion

In 1902 Parker Brothers, already a leading manufacturer of board games, introduced a new parlor game that was not played on a board but on a table divided by a net. It was a version of table tennis, which had been played in various forms for about 20 years, but it was different in one important respect: instead of India rubber the ball was made of Celluloid.

The sound that the light plastic ball produced when it was struck supplied the inspiration for a catchy name: Ping-Pong. As the game graduated from the dining table to a table of its own, it came to be played, not in genteel fashion by long-skirted ladies like the one shown on the box cover at right, but by highly trained and fiercely competitive athletes of both sexes.

The game was an instant success when it first appeared in the United States. The fad lasted some two years before it faded, only to return after about two decades. In the late 1920s popularity reached a peak when millions of players around the country competed for a trophy called the Parker Cup. Since then interest in table tennis as a diversion has

The ball looks familiar but the paddle handle looks a bit long in this 1902 Ping-Pong set. The box holds the net and another bat.

remained high, and in other parts of the world it is widely recognized as a serious sport—surprisingly it enjoys great popularity and status in China. In that nation, a game that began with a name that has an oddly, though unintentionally, Chinese sound is virtually the national sport.

This Parker game board shows U.S. battleships steaming toward Havana Harbor, the goal, under the guns of Spanish fortifications. This patriotic diversion came out in 1898, the year of the Spanish-American War.

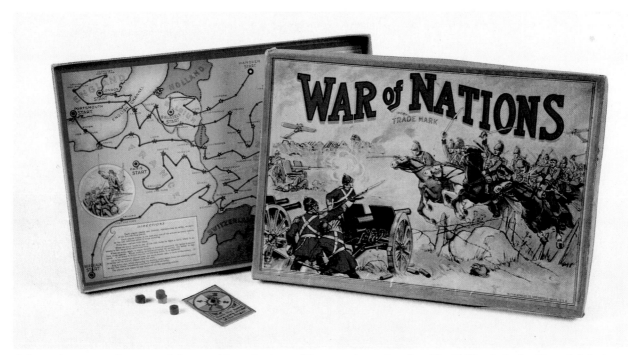

Saber-swinging cavalrymen and fancy uniforms lend an oddly 19th Century flavor to the box cover of a 1918 game that apparently was based on World War I. At the spinner's behest, armies advance and retreat across a battlefield that is a map of Europe.

Based on the premise that policemen compete with one another to catch the largest number of criminals, the 1896 game of Rival Policemen featured a board consisting of a grid of streets along which the policemen were moved to capture counters that represented crooks.

MUSEUMS
The Game Preserve
Peterborough, New Hampshire 03458

Mary Merritt Doll Museum
Douglassville, Pennsylvania 19518

Museum of the City of New York
New York, New York 10029

Perelman Antique Toy Museum
Philadelphia, Pennsylvania 19106

Raggedy Ann Antique Doll and Toy Museum
Flemington, New Jersey 08822

PERIODICALS
Antique Toy World Magazine, 3941 Belle Plains, Chicago, Illinois 60618

BOOKS
Berndt, Frederick, *The Domino Book.* Thomas Nelson, Inc., Publishers, 1974.

Catalogue of McLoughlin Bros. (facsimile). Herbert J. Siegel, P.O. Box 75, Wyncote, Pennsylvania 19095,

originally published 1886.

Freeman, Larry, ed., *Yesterday's Games.* Century House Publishing, Inc., 1970.

Grunfeld, Frederic V., ed., *Games of the World.* Holt, Rinehart and Winston, 1975.

Kaye, Marvin, *The Story of Monopoly, Silly Putty, Bingo, Twister, Frisbee, Scrabble, et cetera.* Stein & Day Publishers, 1973.

McClinton, Katharine Morrison, *Antiques of American Childhood.* Clarkson N. Potter, Inc., 1970.

Mebane, John, *The Coming Collecting Boom.* A. S. Barnes and Co., Inc., 1968.

90 Years of Fun, 1883-1973, The History of Parker Brothers. Parker Brothers, 1973.

Schroeder, Joseph J., Jr., ed., *The Wonderful World of Toys, Games and Dolls, 1860-1930.* Digest Books, Inc., 1971.

Shea, James J., and Charles Mercer, *It's All in the Game.* G. P. Putnam's Sons, 1960.

Golf Clubs
Tools for an Ancient Sport

A young pro who worked at a golf course near New York was browsing around in a thrift shop in 1977 when he spotted an old wooden-headed golf club in a bin of secondhand sticks. It had been painted black. Examining it more closely, he detected under the paint and grime the name Tommy Armour imprinted on the club's head.

The browser knew he had a find: Armour, a well-known golfer of the 1920s and '30s, had licensed the use of his name on certain quality clubs (*opposite*) that have become prizes for collectors—among them sportsmen who use the clubs in actual play. The young professional refinished the wood (brand-new in the early 1950s, it had cost $12) and took it to the nearby Westchester Country Club, where a professional golf tournament was being held. In about 15 minutes he had found a buyer for the refurbished club. The selling price: $350.

That is how valuable some old golf clubs have become. Some enthusiasts search out classic clubs that can still be used in play, such as those bearing the Tommy Armour signature; in the opinion of many, these clubs are better

Joseph Murdoch is co-founder of the Golf Collectors' Society and in 1970 became editor of the Society's bimonthly "Bulletin."

made and they are actually better in play than those produced more recently.

A growing fraternity of other collectors specializes in antique clubs—some made in the 1700s still exist. People also collect old golf balls, wooden tees, early golf bags, pictures, books and magazines—even sand from sand traps. One man I know has collected score cards from 10,000 different courses. Many of the objects so avidly sought, like the Armour clubs, are of relatively recent manufacture, and valuable examples often turn

An 1892 lithograph by the British caricaturist "Lib" captures the sloping walk of John Ball Jr., eight times British amateur champion.

up in thrift shops and garage sales.

There are three categories of collectible golf clubs, corresponding to the three types of ball that have been used: the "featherie" ball, employed from the time the game was invented in Scotland in the 1400s, until 1850; the "guttie," from about 1845 to 1899; and, since the turn of the century, the rubber ball.

The names given the balls derive from the materials used in them. To make a featherie, a ball maker first filled a top hat with loose goose feathers to get the prescribed amount of stuffing. Then he boiled them and stuffed the wet, compacted mess into a pouch of seamed leather strips. When all the feathers were packed, the ball maker sewed up the last seam. After the feathers dried, the sphere became as hard as, well, as a golf ball. The leather cover cut easily, so pre-1850 golfers usually swept the ball off the turf rather than hit it, using slim, light, wooden-headed clubs, or woods. Before 1850 few iron-headed clubs existed.

Pre-1850 woods—the term always refers to the head, for shafts for all clubs were wooden until the 1920s— are the true antiques of golf. The most valuable were made in Scotland before 1850 by Hugh Philp and by three generations of the McEwan family. The Philp clubs are called long nose, their heads are each about 5 inches along the flat striking face—"heel to toe." Philp stamped his name on his club heads (but when he died someone stole his stamp and produced fakes).

The McEwans also marked their clubs. James, who made clubs from 1790 to 1810 in a shop near the now-defunct Musselburg course, outside Edinburgh, often added a thistle design to his name. Clubs made by his

The most valuable classic clubs of the 1930s to 1960s are matched sets. This one is trademarked MacGregor, is signed by pro Tommy Armour and bears the nickname he got for his white hair—Silver Scot.

son Peter and grandson Douglas just read "McEwan." Although three more generations of McEwans made clubs until 1970, they of course did not make long-nose clubs for featheries, and their work is valued less.

Virtually any pre-1850 club is desirable. A shallow face on a wood generally indicates early manufacture, as does a shaft made of ash. Hickory shafts did not come into use until about 1840. Old irons can be identified by examining the hosel, the metal section that attaches the iron head to the wooden shaft. The club is pre-1850 if the hosel has a seam, showing where it was hand-rolled into a cylinder to grasp the shaft. After 1850 hosels were solid iron into which a shaft hole was reamed.

Shortly before 1850 a white ball of rubber-like gutta percha was introduced. Gutties were solid and hard, so hard that hitting them with clubs designed for featheries often broke the club. Club makers began to make the wooden heads thicker from the club face to the back of the head and shorter from heel to toe, which resulted in the "bulldog" shape that most woods still retain.

More irons, such as the niblick and mashie, came into use. The niblick and mashie survive under different names (box, below), but some of the irons fashioned between 1850 and 1900 are no longer made. Collectors seek experiments such as the water mashie (page 65), but any club from the guttie era is desirable.

Age increases value, and can often be determined from the method used to attach head and shaft. In the 19th Century, the joint was strengthened with 5 or 6 inches of whipping—strong thread tightly wound around the joint and then shellacked or tarred. After 1905 less whipping was used. In addition, the face, smooth in the 19th Century, was generally grooved later to give better control over shots.

By the time clubs with grooved faces became common a new ball of wound rubber strips in a rubber cover—essentially the ball of today—had superseded the guttie. Finally, in the 1920s, steel shafts were introduced.

In the late 1930s club manufacturers began to produce the steel-shafted woods and irons now considered classics. The leading maker was Crawford, McGregor & Canby Company, whose clubs are trademarked MacGregor—a spelling apparently intended to add a more Scottish flavor. A set of eight matched MacGregor irons marked Tommy Armour Silver Scot and numbered 2 through 9, with model number 985 stamped on them, cost under $70 new, in the 1950s. In the '70s such sets were selling at $350 and up. You can tell if the clubs are matched by finding the Registered Number on the head or hosel. This number should be on all the clubs.

Other valuable Armour iron sets include models 945, 915, 925 and 985/160. Also coveted are single examples of Armour clubs: the Ironmaster putter and the Armour 159 wedge—a thick, heavy iron. Armour woods by MacGregor are also sought, especially those with solid persimmon heads, marked "Oil Hardened"; in 1978, a 1950 Tommy Armour model 693 driver sold for $800.

There are various non-Armour irons by MacGregor that are also prized by collectors: sets with a copper tinge on the club faces, the CF 4000 models with black faces, MT (MacGregor Tourney) clubs with small faces and VIP clubs endorsed by the noted golfer of the 1960s and '70s, Jack Nicklaus, marked "By Nicklaus."

MacGregor does not have a monopoly on classics. Among others of increasing value are A. G. Spalding Bros.' Top Flite Synchro-Dyned irons from 1953 and 1954 and Hillerich & Bradsby's Power Bilt drivers, also from the '50s. Among putters that have brought high sums are those of the Sportsman Co., which are stamped Geo. Low Wizard 600, the Thos. E. Wilson Co. R-20 and R-90 wedges, and two Wilson putters: model 8802 and the model marked with the name of pro Arnold Palmer.

To help identify the valuable clubs, old books, magazines and sporting-goods catalogues are useful. One landmark book is Golf, an instruction manual published by Spalding in 1893. This book, now very rare, was put out in the hope of increasing the market for golf equipment. The hope seems to have been fulfilled: there were 13.5 million players in the U.S. alone in 1976, equipment sales topped $631 million a year—and there were plenty of people willing to spend $500 in the belief that a Geo. Low Wizard would improve their chances of stroking a small white sphere into a hole in the ground.

The Old Names: Driver to Niblick

Until the 1930s golf clubs were identified by curious old Scottish names such as mashie or spoon, but since then a numerical system has taken over; the box below matches the old designations (capital letters) with the new. The lower the number, the more nearly vertical the striking face and the flatter and longer the trajectory of the ball. Not listed are three unnumbered clubs: the pitching wedge, a club that was unknown to the old Scots and is intended for high, short pitches to the green; the sand wedge, for use in traps; and the putter, a flat-faced club designed to gentle the ball into the hole once the other weapons have got it to the green.

DRIVER (OR PLAY CLUB): 1-wood	MID MASHIE: 3-iron
BRASSIE: 2-wood	MASHIE IRON: 4-iron
SPOON: 3-wood	MASHIE: 5-iron
BAFFY: 4-wood	SPADE MASHIE: 6-iron
	MASHIE NIBLICK: 7-iron
DRIVING IRON: 1-iron	PITCHING NIBLICK: 8-iron
MIDIRON: 2-iron	NIBLICK: 9-iron

Four balls tell the history of golf. A pre-1850 leather-covered featherie is at left, a guttie, used between 1845 and 1900, at right. A rubber ball (bottom) made around 1900 resembles the modern type (top).

Some golf collectors specialize in score cards. Above are an Allston, Massachusetts, card of the 1890s, a card signed by golfing great Arnold Palmer, and three from prestigious clubs near Philadelphia.

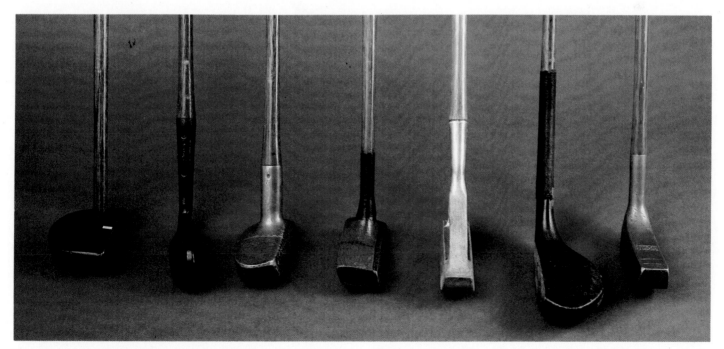

The wide variety in putter designs is illustrated by these seven. From left they are a 1923 Kempshall, a rare 1910 MacGregor, a Schenectady made in that city in 1904 by A. W. Knight, a 1908 putter named for the famous Australian golfer W. J. Travis, a 1920 club by Otto Hackbarth, an 1885 wooden putter—a real rarity—made by Robert Simpson for a left-handed player, and a 1920 Kismet.

An antique wood made by master club maker
Douglas McEwan about 1840 for a featherie
has the long, graceful head of the early clubs.

Below is a small-faced club called a track iron,
used in the early 19th Century to hit a ball off
a road crossing the course or out of a rut—
places a ball is no longer considered playable.

In this rare American-made club from about
1900, head and shaft are made from one piece
of wood, instead of being crafted separately.

This rakelike water mashie dates from the 1890s, when a golfer had to play a ball lying in casual water—golfers' lingo for puddle. Today such a ball is lifted by hand.

A concave wedge, endorsed by golfing great Walter Hagen—who used it to extricate himself from sand traps—was produced for only one year, 1929, then was declared illegal.

A rare iron called a cran cleek was made by Spalding between 1904 and 1920. It has a wood insert in the face to give the ball the spring it would have from a wooden club.

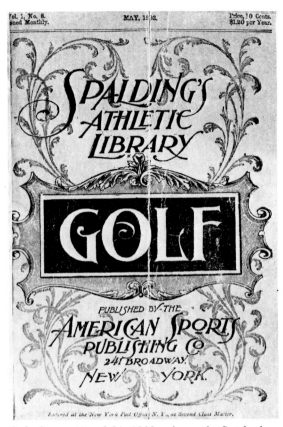

Only three copies of this 1893 volume, the first book on golf published in the U.S., are known to exist.

The oldest golfing magazine began publication in 1890, changing its name to "Golf Illustrated" in 1899.

Women were enthusiastic players by the turn of the century, when this handsome instruction book was put out.

The golf craze of the 1920s prompted the old "Life," a humor magazine, to publish a special issue each year spoofing the game.

An 1889 etching by George Aikman portrays the undulating, treeless Old Course in St. Andrews, Scotland, the world's oldest 18-hole golf course.

MUSEUMS
The American Golf Hall of Fame
Foxburg Country Club
Foxburg, Pennsylvania 16036

United States Golf Association, Golf House
Far Hills, New Jersey 07931

The World Golf Hall of Fame
Pinehurst, North Carolina 28374

COLLECTORS ORGANIZATIONS
Golf Collectors' Society
638 Wagner Road
Lafayette Hill, Pennsylvania 19444

BOOKS
Golf Magazine's *Encyclopedia of Golf.* Harper and Row, 1972.

Good wishes

The Star of Love upon thee shine with changeless radiance, the wine, the music-flowers of life be thine

Fiore

HEAVEN GIVE YOU MANY MANY MERRY DAYS.

Greeting Cards
A Gallery of Best Wishes

When I went to England in 1959 to search for a Christmas card more than 100 years old, my quest received surprising publicity, and the British Broadcasting Corporation asked me to make a radio talk. I took the opportunity to offer £100 (then almost $300) for an undamaged specimen. This card, the first ever published, had caused a furor—it was denounced for fostering drunkenness because its picture of a family toasting the season with wine included children *(page 70).*

After my talk, hundreds of calls poured into the BBC studios. Most responses led only to specimens of a facsimile edition published in 1955. However, one led me to an original, unused and in perfect condition, one of the dozen or so examples surviving out of a printing of 1,000; their value reaches into the thousands of dollars apiece.

Fortunately, however, only the rarest of the antique greeting cards are worth even a fraction of that price;

Carroll Alton Means began collecting cards in 1930, when they were generally ignored, because of a bit of family history: decades earlier his mother and aunts had assembled cards at home for a card manufacturer.

---

many interesting old cards can be purchased for a few dollars or less at church rummage sales, estate auctions and garage sales. And collections can even be started with absolutely no expenditure, because in the decades around the turn of the century many people lovingly preserved the greeting cards they received in albums and scrapbooks. There are undoubtedly millions of old cards that are lying undiscovered in chests, trunks and

Identification of this card as a winner in L. Prang & Co.'s design competition appears on the reverse (above). The prize face is at left.

A fussy still life, busy with patterns typical of Victorian times, decorates the face of the card at left, which bears Christmas and New Year's greetings on the reverse (above). It was produced by L. Prang & Co., a Roxbury, Massachusetts, lithography firm renowned for color printing, and it won a prize that Prang, like other publishers, offered artists.

shoe boxes in the attics of America.

Most collectors of old cards stick to Christmas and New Year's messages. Some people also include valentines (which are discussed in a separate article in this encyclopedia) and humorous cards.

Those who collect cards issued after 1900 add greetings in honor of Easter and Thanksgiving, first issued in quantity around 1908, and a growing number of collectors now search for ingenious novelty cards with movable parts. Most collectors keep the birthday cards they find in their search for holiday messages but do not include Mother's Day cards and sympathy cards, which became popular only after World War I. The most important find a collector can make is an old publisher's sample book—a seasonal or annual sales-promotion device displaying the maker's then-current line.

One reason that very first card, designed by John Calcott Horsley and published by his friend Henry Cole, is so valuable is its status as a maverick. It did not establish the greeting-card business; only a few others appeared sporadically for nearly 20 years. Then, in 1860, the British publisher Charles Goodall & Son got into greeting cards by way of another kind of card: the one used for visiting. At that time middle- and upper-class people paid formal calls on friends, and it was customary to leave a visiting card as a reminder of the visit. Goodall began to produce cards designed for visits at Christmas. These were generally small, little more than 2 by 3 inches; they were brightly colored and some were decorated with simple designs, such as holly. From Christmas visiting cards it was a short and logical step to a card sent ahead of time to carry the season's greetings—perhaps someone at Goodall recalled Henry Cole's experiment.

The most sought-after cards are those made between 1860 and the 1890s by Goodall and the competitors its success attracted—Marcus Ward & Co., De La Rue & Co. and Raphael Tuck & Co. (later Raphael Tuck &

Sons) in England, and L. Prang & Co. in America. The English cards were imported to the United States in large quantities, so that they now are found in America as readily as domestic ones of the same period.

The 19th Century cards are the most desirable because they are generally the most beautiful—carefully and expensively printed by the old-fashioned lithography process to reproduce charmingly colorful illustrations by popular artists of the time. The most famous artist by far was Kate Greenaway, later celebrated as an illustrator of children's books, who worked mainly for Marcus Ward & Co. Her round-eyed children with solemn countenances became Victorian favorites. Greenaway cards sold so well that they were widely imitated. Perhaps half of all cards featuring children drawn between 1870 and 1900 were designed by Greenaway or her imitators. She did not sign her earliest work, but most of her later Marcus Ward cards bear her initials.

Other major firms also employed prominent artists, many of them women. The most successful De La Rue artists were William and Rebecca Coleman, a brother-and-sister team—Rebecca did portraits of girls, William created innocent-looking nudes. Raphael Tuck commis-

sioned Royal Academy artists to design Christmas cards.

In America the outstanding 19th Century cardmaker was Louis Prang, a German immigrant who began to produce Christmas cards in 1874 at his Roxbury, Massachusetts, printing plant. Prang went to great lengths in transforming his artists' paintings into faithful and sometimes stunning reproductions: to print one of his more elaborate cards took more than 20 plates. Because of the care lavished on manufacture, Prang's cards even in the 1880s cost as much as $1, a large sum for the time. They are valuable today, especially those with a date.

In the mid-1890s the greeting-card market became flooded with less expensive cards, many made in Germany, and most of the old-line firms went out of business. Of the new wave of cards, collectors value the so-called mechanicals, which have parts that move or pop up. Because of their fragile construction, few old mechanicals have survived intact; those that did are valuable. No one firm dominated the market, but cards made by Meggendorfer of Munich are desirable.

Besides mechanicals, other novelty cards that interest collectors are ingeniously designed cards in which smiling faces, when turned upside down, turn to scowls, and

The first commercial Christmas and New Year's card (above), printed in London in 1843, is very rare, but copies of a facsimile reprint issued in 1955 can be found. This original, in perfect condition, was located in England by the collector for the Hallmark Historical Collection.

landscapes, when turned 90°, become portraits. Also collectible are cards imitating paper money or bank notes, drawn from a "bank" of love for such sums as a "thousand good wishes"; they were so realistic that they were easily mistaken for genuine cash and eventually were banned by government authorities. Other valuable cards portrayed mundane items—ashtrays, shoelaces and dishes—in three dimensions and were displayed on the mantel as knickknacks by their recipients. Scented cards are sought, as well as cards with sound effects—one had a noisemaker hidden between two sheets of cardboard, so that it chirped like a bird when pressed.

Early examples from modern American card publishers, such as The Gibson Art Company, Rust Craft Greeting Cards, Inc., and Hallmark Cards, Inc., are also prized. Noted ones are hand-painted, smaller than a present-day government postcard, issued in 1915 by what was then Hall Brothers, and two Rust Craft novelties—folding Christmas cards issued from 1906, and Tukkins, tiny cards inserted in a larger one.

For related material, see the article on Valentines in a separate volume of this encyclopedia.

A 19th Century Christmas card with paper lace looks like a valentine. Paper lace was a favorite embellishment on Victorian cards.

An early New Year's card, reproduced here larger than it is in actuality, was published by Charles Goodall & Son of London, the pioneer in mass production of greeting cards. Just larger than 2 by 3 inches, it resembles the decorated visiting cards, which were forerunners of greeting cards.

The cards on these two pages were designed by Kate Greenaway, a leading Victorian illustrator, and issued by Marcus Ward & Co., which achieved top ranking largely because of Greenaway's popularity. A matched set of Greenaway designs, like the four above, is a collector's prize—to assemble a set, a collector must match borders, sizes and also greetings. The square cards below were issued both as separate cards and as a set that folded like a bellows. At right is an all-occasion card with the artist's initials in the lower left corner, under the inscription.

A VERY HAPPY NEW YEAR TO YOU.

WITH THE BEST OF GOOD WISHES.

TO WISH YOU A MERRY CHRISTMAS.

GREETING

Merry Christmas for Papa

Artists for many 19th Century publishers imitated Kate Greenaway, as in these examples from Raphael Tuck & Sons of London. Greenaway's style, readily identified by huge, innocent eyes and Cupid's-bow lips, still remains popular in the commercial art of the 20th Century.

Two newly hatched bees are serenaded by fiddling grasshoppers on the birthday card at right, while a decorously nude swimmer admires butterflies on the Christmas card below—typical of the totally irrelevant scenes that decorated many Victorian cards. The nude was the work of William Coleman, who along with his sister Rebecca drew pictures for De La Rue & Co., the British firm that published both cards reproduced here.

JOYOUS AND GRACIOUS BE THY CHRISTMAS DAY!

Fourth Prize Design.

With the Season's Greetings.

S. Hildesheimer & Co. of London issued the card above, which won fourth prize in one of its annual Christmas-card design competitions. Seaside scenes like this one were quite popular in the late 19th Century.

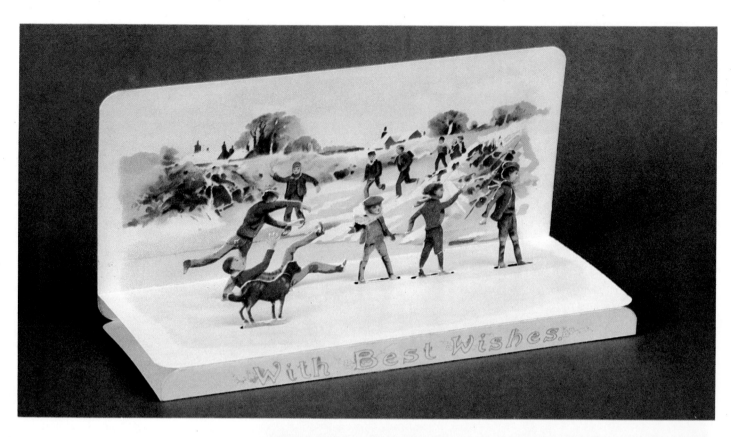

Late-19th and early-20th Century novelty cards are very desirable, particularly if in perfect condition, as these are—they are so fragile, few have survived undamaged. Above is an English pop-up put out for Christmas 1890; when the card is opened, the skating figures spring up to make a sort of diorama. The Easter card at right, which was printed in Germany about 1910, unfolds to create a bas-relief pail and well for the flat printed eggs.

Reproduced on these pages are four kinds of the expensive cards issued by L. Prang & Co., foremost American card publisher of the 19th Century. Opposite at top are Christmas and New Year's angels and cherubs in a long format, unusual for the time. The New Year's greeting at left could be folded like a booklet and tied with tassels. The square shape of the Christmas cards above is unusual, but the brown suit Santa wears is not—in the 19th Century he was pictured in blue, red, gold, purple, green, brown or black. The Thanksgiving card at right is rare because such cards did not become popular until after 1908.

Thanksgiving Greetings

We're to think of our blessings
Before this day ends,
But there's no time limit
For thinking of friends.

BIRTHDAY CONSOLATIONS

Another year! Ain't it the truth
We're getting further from our youth?
Don't cry, old dear,
Whate'er you do;
Just lie, old dear—
I'll stand by you.

Cards from the 1920s and 1930s, like the examples shown here, are scarce because by that time the Victorian pastime of preserving greetings in scrapbooks had lost favor. These mint-condition survivors, typical of designs of the period, came from a stationery store that had been closed with stock intact for more than 40 years. The ones above and at top right are from Rust Craft; the other two are unmarked.

MUSEUMS
American Antiquarian Society
Worcester, Massachusetts 01609

The New-York Historical Society
New York, New York 10024

Worcester Historical Society
Worcester, Massachusetts 01608

COLLECTORS ORGANIZATIONS
Prang-Mark Society
Old Irelandville
Watkins Glen, New York 14891

BOOKS
Buday, George, *The History of the Christmas Card.*
Spring Books, 1954.

Chase, Ernest Dudley, *The Romance of Greeting Cards.* Tower Books, 1971.

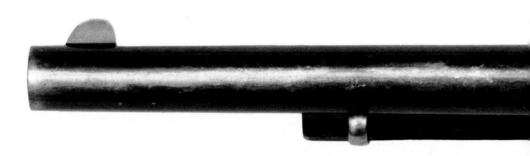

Guns
Firearms that Made History

T he Continental Army rifleman stretched out on the grass, aimed almost nonchalantly at the three British cavalrymen on the far side of the field, and fired. The rifle ball whistled between the two officers, killing their bugler's horse. "I think," said Major George Hanger to Colonel Banastre Tarleton, "that we had better move, or we shall have two or three of these gentlemen shortly amusing themselves at our expense."

When Hanger got back to England after the Revolution, he voiced considerable respect for the marksman-

Ronald Bullock, an attorney in New York state, has served as president of the Mid-State Arms Collectors and Shooters Club and has been active in organizing gun shows for collectors in the northeastern United States.

ship of the Americans, and similar admiration was expressed for the accurate, long-range rifles their snipers used. But not for many decades did weapons of similar range and accuracy supplant the crude firearms of earlier times. Then gradually guns were introduced that could shoot farther, faster and straighter; they transformed warfare during the 19th Century. That array of weapons also has been attracting collectors ever since.

Landmark designs, weapons associated with historical events, and examples of unusual craftsmanship—all catch the attention of gun enthusiasts. Some search for pistols or rifles only; others seek products of a particular manufacturer, or even different versions of one particular gun—I have seven models of the Winchester Model 1873, "the gun that won the West." One popular way to specialize is to collect by period—relics from the 18th Century or earlier are costly, Civil War guns less so and World War II souvenirs relatively inexpensive.

The technological advances dividing one period from another began with rifling—grooves inside the barrel that spin the bullet, making it travel straighter and farther than the ball from the smooth musket bore. The American rifle that impressed British officers was a type made by Germans who settled Lancaster County, Pennsylvania, around 1720. They redesigned their hunting rifles, lengthening the barrels to improve accuracy and range, and narrowing them to preserve powder.

Before long, guns such as these were in widespread use among settlers in Ohio, the Carolinas, Virginia and the other frontier states. The settlers knew the gun as

The Colt Peacemaker reproduced on these pages is rare because of its long barrel (7 ½ inches), its age (it was produced in August 1878) and its excellent condition. Several hundred thousand Peacemakers of various models were manufactured, the last ones in 1972.

the long rifle; it came to be called a Kentucky rifle because of a song commemorating General Andrew Jackson's victory at New Orleans in the War of 1812:

But Jackson he was wide awake, and wasn't scar'd at trifles,
For well he knew what aim we take, with our Kentucky rifles.

The Kentucky rifle was basically a hunting weapon, however, and most military guns had smoothbore barrels until the Civil War. Thus collectors of Revolutionary guns look not only for Kentuckies but for Charleville muskets, supplied by the French to the rebellious Colonies, and for British Brown Bess muskets.

After 1777, the Revolutionary American government stamped "US" or "U States" on its guns, and examples with these markings are especially valuable. The first guns made for the United States were pistols, now rare, made in 1799 by Simeon North and Elisha Cheney of Berlin, Connecticut, and marked "North & Cheney Berlin" or "S. North & E. Cheney Berlin." Easier to find are weapons from America's first armories in Springfield, Massachusetts, and Harpers Ferry, West Virginia.

Springfields were unmarked from 1795 to 1798, but those made from 1799 onward have the armory name on them, as do those from Harpers Ferry made from 1800 onward. Also highly collectible among guns of this period are those made by the versatile Eli Whitney, best known for inventing the cotton gin. In New Haven, Connecticut, Whitney and his descendants made guns from 1798 to 1888, and their products, marked "New Haven" or "N. Haven," are a category in themselves.

A relative of the Kentucky that collectors look for is the New England Kentucky, made in and near Worcester, Massachusetts, at the turn of the century. It has its own distinctive features—a pointed projection in front of the trigger guard and a silver escutcheon plate near the cheek rest. Another Kentucky variant, first made by the Hawken brothers of St. Louis around 1820, is known as the buffalo, plains or mountain rifle. The barrel was shortened for use by mounted hunters, and the bore enlarged to take a bigger charge for bigger game.

Most of these weapons—rifles, muskets and pistols—were flintlock muzzle-loaders. Loose gunpowder and bullets were pushed down the muzzle, and the powder was ignited by a spark from a flint. About 1840, a better ignition system was found using caps—like those for toy guns, each containing a small amount of easily detonated explosive—instead of flints. When struck by the hammer of the gun, the cap exploded through a nipple on the side of the gun to set off the main charge. Such percussion guns were less apt to misfire, and many flintlocks were converted, lowering their value to collectors.

Original percussions are very much sought after. The first percussion pistol ordered by the U.S. government, for example, the Model 1842, was made by three manufacturers; those from the Palmetto Armory in Columbia, South Carolina, are the rarest. The last muzzleloader made for the U.S. armed forces, the Model 1864 percussion rifle, is another one that collectors prize.

The most famous American gunmaker to make his appearance during the percussion period was Samuel Colt, and he came to the business with *élan*. At age eight, he was sneaking away from church to practice firing his father's musket. At 14, he exploded a homemade bomb in the village pond; the blast shattered the windows of surrounding homes and spooked the team of horses pulling a coach occupied by President John Quincy Adams, injuring the coachman. At about 15 Colt was expelled from Amherst after an experiment with explosives set fire to a school building. At 16, he was on his way to India as a deck hand. At about 17 he was back in the United States as the proprietor of a traveling show. At the age of 22 he started making guns.

With borrowed money Colt opened a factory in Paterson, New Jersey, and began to make his famous Patersons. There were eight basic models, from rifles to small pocket weapons, but Colt's fame rests on his pioneering revolvers, pistols with a revolving cylinder that enabled them to fire more than one shot without reloading.

Colt's guns sold well, but the way he did his selling—throwing in free guns for Army purchasing officers, for example—horrified family investors. They pulled out of the enterprise and Colt went bankrupt. Six years after the opening of his factory, Colt—or "Dr. Coult late of New York, London and Calcutta," as his handbills proclaimed—was back on the road with his traveling show. In 1847, government orders for the Mexican War put Colt back in the gun business, most notably with the huge Colt Walker, named after Captain Sam Walker of the Texas Rangers, who contributed to its design.

The percussion guns Colt and others made in the middle of the century, all front-loading, were soon rendered obsolete by a still newer system: the cartridge. The detonator, propelling charge and shot all were encased in a single tube, first made of paper, later metal. The cartridge fired when the hammer struck the casing over the chemical, and the tube contained all the blast.

By the time of the Civil War, a period that provides a variety of popular collectibles (see the article on Civil War Equipment in a separate volume of this encyclopedia), most of the features of modern guns had been developed. Weapons were available that were loaded with cartridges to fire repeatedly through rifled barrels, and some of these saw combat. But so did every other kind of weapon, and the value of a gun as a Civil War memento depends on evidence of actual use then.

Civil War collectors specialize, many of them narrowly. An increasingly popular category is the matériel manufactured in the Confederacy, such as the rifles

Decorative Holders for Gunpowder

So long as guns had to be loaded by pouring powder and shot separately into the muzzle—until the late 1850s—something was needed to carry gunpowder. Cattle horns were easily obtainable, tough and waterproof, and they were conveniently shaped for pouring powder. Many gunpowder horns were elaborately engraved, and good specimens are quite desirable today.

Among the more valuable of the old powder horns are those bearing maps—in many cases the maps were not simply decoration but were meant to be used *(bottom)*. Also sought after are horns carved with reflections of their owners—religious, patriotic or personal. "Valley Forge, sick, damit," a Revolutionary War soldier named Val Prentice inscribed on his powder horn.

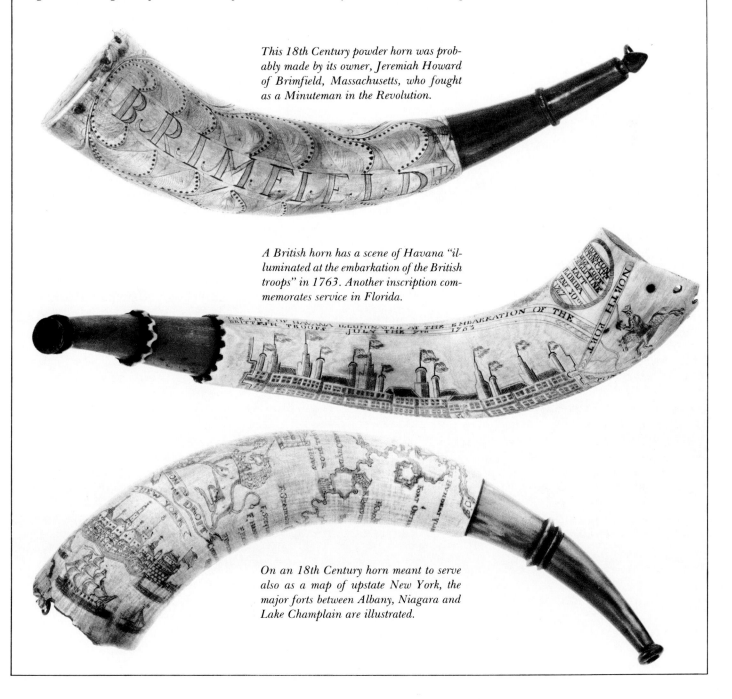

This 18th Century powder horn was probably made by its owner, Jeremiah Howard of Brimfield, Massachusetts, who fought as a Minuteman in the Revolution.

A British horn has a scene of Havana "illuminated at the embarkation of the British troops" in 1763. Another inscription commemorates service in Florida.

On an 18th Century horn meant to serve also as a map of upstate New York, the major forts between Albany, Niagara and Lake Champlain are illustrated.

made by the Fayetteville Armory in North Carolina. The lock plates of these guns are marked "Fayetteville" or "Fayetteville, N.C.," and an eagle and "C.S.A." usually appear someplace on each. Another interesting class takes in handguns put together in the South from parts captured from the Union arsenal at Harpers Ferry. One bears the Fayetteville mark and the date, but if the date is after 1862 the gun is a fake, for the Harpers Ferry parts ran out in that year and production stopped. Many old handguns were repaired and put into working order for the Confederacy by a number of gunsmiths. A gunsmith to look for is Samuel Sutherland of Richmond, "Armorer of the South." Guns he fixed bear his initials, "S. S.," and sometimes also "Richmond."

After the Civil War, the United States turned its energies to the challenge of the West. Guns were everyday gear, and new developments that had seen limited use in the War, such as rapid-firing, cartridge-loading revolvers and repeating rifles, became common arms. The manufacturers' names most often associated with this period are Winchester, Colt (though Samuel had died in 1862) and, to a lesser degree, Remington.

Oliver Winchester, a former shirtmaker, had bought and sold the controlling interest in several gun companies before organizing his Winchester Repeating Arms Company, most famous for the Model 1873 rifle, in which a lever behind the trigger ejects a spent cartridge, positions a fresh one in the breech and cocks the weapon for firing. A simpler rifle made by Remington is less valued by collectors, although the Frontier model, used by the American Indian police on reservations, is desirable.

The handgun most associated with the West is the Colt Single Action Army Revolver—the famous Peacemaker. The first Colt made for cartridges, it followed a design pioneered earlier by Smith & Wesson. It was manufactured from 1872 until 1940 in a variety of calibers (barrel diameters) for military and civilian use. Collectors place great value on Army Peacemakers that have the original blue metal finish, and they also prize models with decorative engraving and fancy grips.

The Peacemaker came into being at a time when the search for fully automatic firearms intensified and began to yield results. The idea had been around since the 18th Century, but was not realized until Richard Jordan Gatling perfected the gun that bears his name *(pages 98 and 99)* during the Civil War.

The Gatling had to be cranked by hand, so that it was not totally machine-operated. The first true machine gun—that is, one that keeps firing as long as the trigger is depressed—was invented in 1883 in England by Hi-

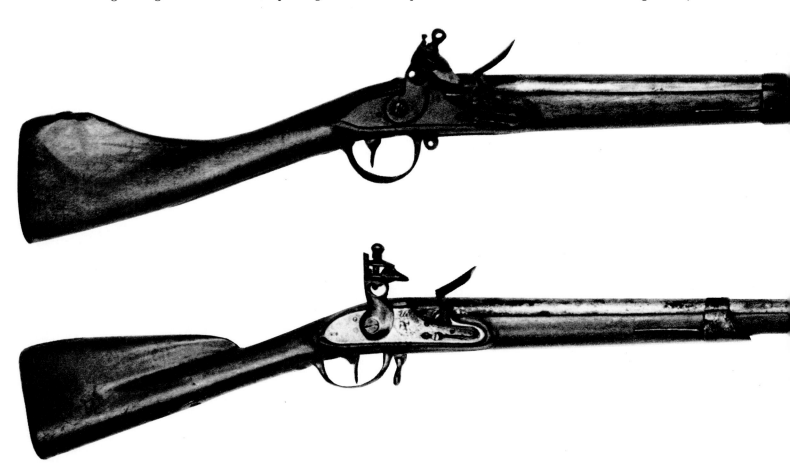

ram Maxim. Soon after, German inventors produced the first semiautomatic pistols—the Borchardt in 1893 and the more famous Luger in 1898. (Such pistols are commonly but incorrectly called automatics; unlike true automatics, which fire repeatedly like machine guns, semiautomatics fire once for each pull of the trigger, then reset themselves for the next shot.) American manufacturers quickly caught up. In 1900 Colt issued the first of a variety sought today. The most famous is Model 1911, made in huge quantities for more than 50 years.

World War I was an all-too-bloody testing ground for many new weapons, but only recently have they begun to attract collectors. On the other hand, World War II weapons seem to have become collectible even before the War ended. The M-1, a semiautomatic carbine, the Colt Model 1911 and the Reising submachine gun, used widely by Marines in the South Pacific—all instantly became collectors' prizes and remain so today.

A serious problem for collectors is a web of federal, state and local laws. Antiques are usually exempt, but federal law defines antique guns as those made before 1899, while in North Dakota an antique gun is one more than 50 years old, and New York City's cutoff is 1894.

Regulation of modern guns is even more confusing. Ownership of fully automatic guns in operating condi-

tion is illegal in all states. Handguns generally are more severely restricted than rifles and shotguns. The strictest laws apply in the Northeast, and certain metropolitan centers, like New York City and Washington, D.C., impose local restrictions on top of state and federal laws. As a result, it is important for anyone collecting guns to keep himself fully informed on all the regulations that apply in his own area; the best way to do this is to get in touch with the National Rifle Association (page 99).

The existence of so many laws concerning ownership of guns is understandable, for guns are potentially the most lethal of all collectibles. They also can be among the most instructive to the student of their history. The Gatling gun is a good example. Most commanders reserved it for such stationary defensive work as guarding bridges, ignoring its value as a mobile assault weapon, even though it was mounted on wheels. In 1876, one notably misguided American Cavalry general made that error. Sure that his battery of Gatlings would be of no use to him on a patrol of hostile Indian territory, General George Armstrong Custer left them behind when he cantered off to Little Bighorn and the pages of history.

For related material, see articles on Civil War Equipment and Cowboy Gear in separate volumes of this encyclopedia.

A concave curve has been carved out of the butt of a Revolutionary War soldier's musket, a French-made Model 1763 Charleville, which originally looked like the Springfield below. Modifications, probably made by the soldiers using the weapons, are often found on 18th Century guns.

The U.S. Army's first American-made gun, modeled on the Charleville (top), was also the first of many to bear the name of the Springfield Armory in Massachusetts. It was introduced in 1795, but it was not until 1799 that date, armory name and identifying eagle were stamped on.

A Kentucky rifle (above), made about 1820, is distinctive for its "tiger stripe"—the grain pattern in its maple stock—and the brass fittings of its patch-box cover, butt plate, trigger guard and nose cap. The original flintlock firing system has been converted to use percussion caps.

The basic design of the Kentucky rifle is retained in this later version, made originally as a percussion type in southwestern New York about 1850. The barrel was cut down after manufacture to reduce weight. The walnut stock has a brass-lidded recess for storing loading patches.

"The gun that won the West"—Winchester's famous Model 1873 15-shot repeating rifle—came in a variety of calibers, lengths, barrel shapes, sights and stocks; above is a .38-40, 24-inch octagonal. More than 700,000 were produced between 1873 and 1919, and many survive.

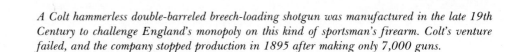

A Colt hammerless double-barreled breech-loading shotgun was manufactured in the late 19th Century to challenge England's monopoly on this kind of sportsman's firearm. Colt's venture failed, and the company stopped production in 1895 after making only 7,000 guns.

Matched pistols and rifle—silver- and gold-inlaid flint-locks—are the work of Nicolas Noël Boutet of France, whose name appears on the barrels. On the lower pistol a plate is marked "Nicolai Shabelski," the man to whom the set is believed to have been presented by Napoleon.

Weapons to be Admired More than Fired

Guns made with decorations so opulent that they could be taken to be works of master jewelers rather than of gunsmiths have been made all over the world practically since the invention of firearms. These elaborate weapons are presentation pieces. Traditional marksmanship prizes and gifts to kings and retired heroes, they were workable but not meant to be used—"adornments of gold and silver, certain to catch the sunlight and cast glare into the shooter's aim, rendered them dangerous if not useless," commented the modern authority Robert Held.

The most renowned maker of presentation guns was Nicolas Noël Boutet, technical director of the French state armory at Versailles, who was in charge of producing military weapons as well as gifts *(above)* during the turbulent times of Louis XVI, the Revolutionary *Directoire* and Napoleon. A pair of Boutet pistols brought almost $10,000 in 1970.

Guns made in the 18th Century by such English gunsmiths as James Freeman *(opposite, top)* and Louis Barbar also are sought after. So are pieces made by the Markhardt brothers, Simon and Peter, who were lured from Germany to Spain by King Charles V in the 16th Century, and by the Kuchenreuter family, which provided guns for the noble Thurn and Taxis families of Germany for a number of generations, in the late 17th Century.

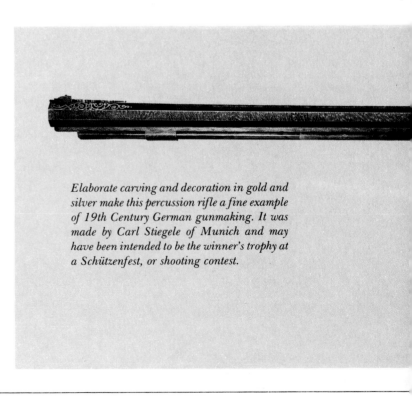

Elaborate carving and decoration in gold and silver make this percussion rifle a fine example of 19th Century German gunmaking. It was made by Carl Stiegele of Munich and may have been intended to be the winner's trophy at a Schützenfest, or shooting contest.

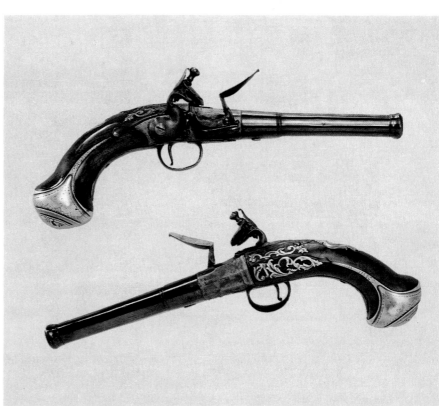

The extremely rare pair of silver-mounted officer's pistols above was made around 1725 by James Freeman, a leading English gunsmith of the period. The butts of the guns have grips in the shape of fishtails, and the barrels can be screwed off to load for firing.

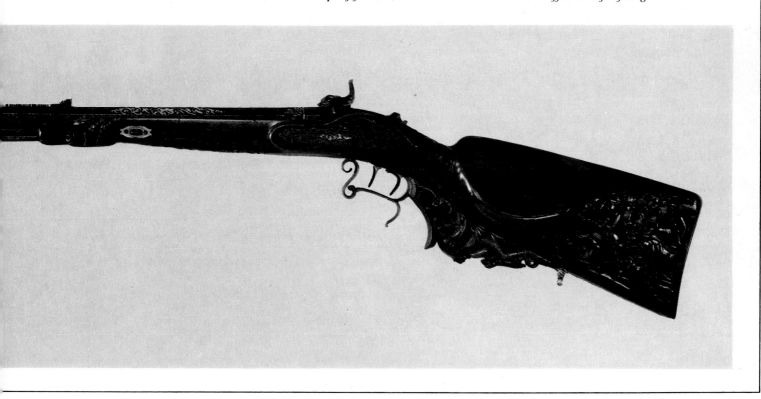

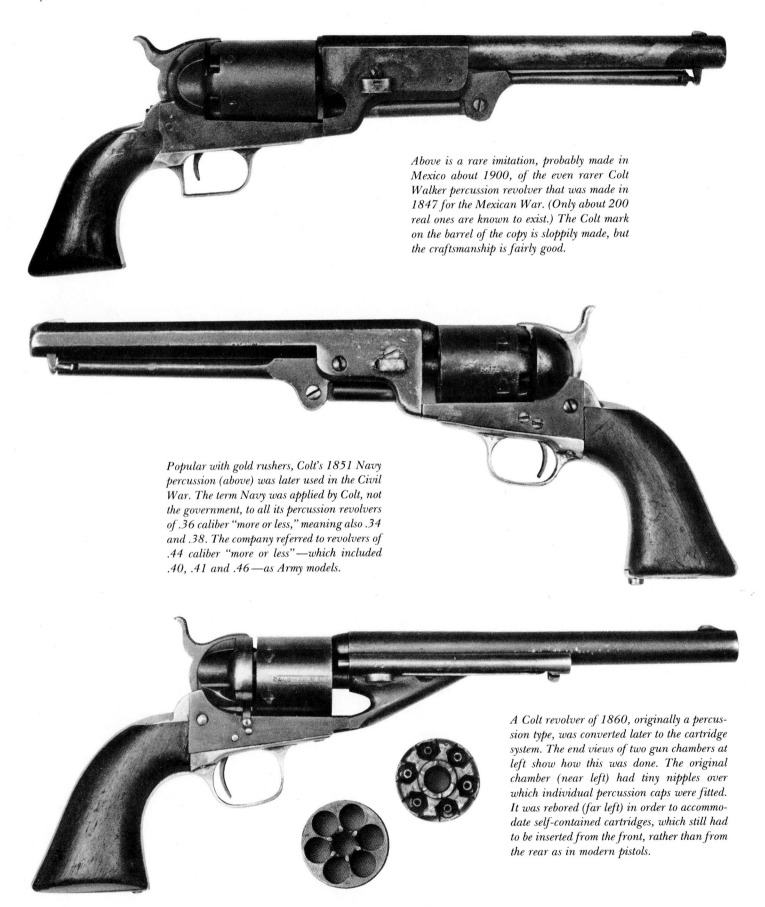

Above is a rare imitation, probably made in Mexico about 1900, of the even rarer Colt Walker percussion revolver that was made in 1847 for the Mexican War. (Only about 200 real ones are known to exist.) The Colt mark on the barrel of the copy is sloppily made, but the craftsmanship is fairly good.

Popular with gold rushers, Colt's 1851 Navy percussion (above) was later used in the Civil War. The term Navy was applied by Colt, not the government, to all its percussion revolvers of .36 caliber "more or less," meaning also .34 and .38. The company referred to revolvers of .44 caliber "more or less"—which included .40, .41 and .46—as Army models.

A Colt revolver of 1860, originally a percussion type, was converted later to the cartridge system. The end views of two gun chambers at left show how this was done. The original chamber (near left) had tiny nipples over which individual percussion caps were fitted. It was rebored (far left) in order to accommodate self-contained cartridges, which still had to be inserted from the front, rather than from the rear as in modern pistols.

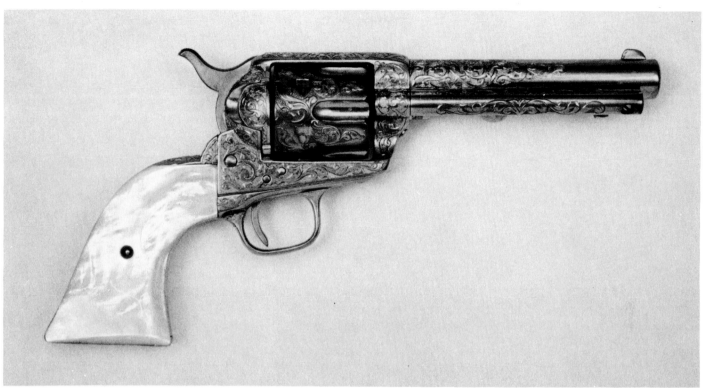

Mother-of-pearl grips, a gold and nickel finish, and elaborate engraving make this .45-caliber Model 1873 Peacemaker very rare. Colt offered these revolvers with perhaps a thousand variations on the basic model (pages 82-83), including a choice of some 30 different calibers.

The Colt trademark, a rampant young horse visible on the rubber grip of the Lightning .38 above, first appeared in 1872. The Lightning was the company's first double-action revolver—it could be fired without first being cocked. This gun is in working condition and therefore rare.

The original velvet-lined case makes this Smith & Wesson .22 valuable—117,000 Model No. 1 Second Issue revolvers were made from 1860 to 1868, and the gun is fairly common. The patent number for the cartridge—a Smith & Wesson innovation—is on the cylinder.

Innumerable "suicide specials" were sold for a dollar or so in the late 19th Century, making it easy to kill oneself or, alternatively, be killed by accident. The early ones were cheap guns like Lee Arms's Red Jacket at top, but the term later applied to any pocket-sized pistol, such as the high-quality Smith & Wesson above.

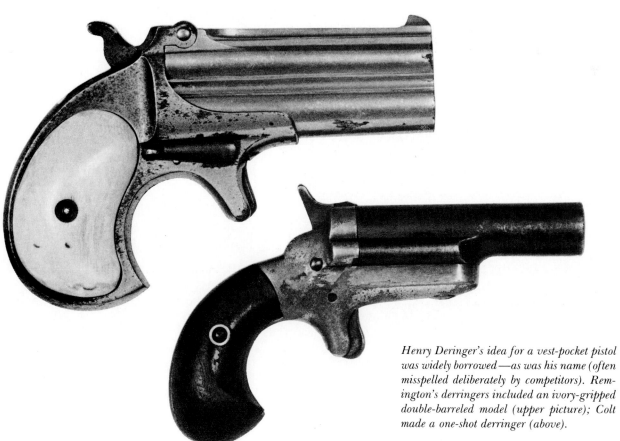

Henry Deringer's idea for a vest-pocket pistol was widely borrowed—as was his name (often misspelled deliberately by competitors). Remington's derringers included an ivory-gripped double-barreled model (upper picture); Colt made a one-shot derringer (above).

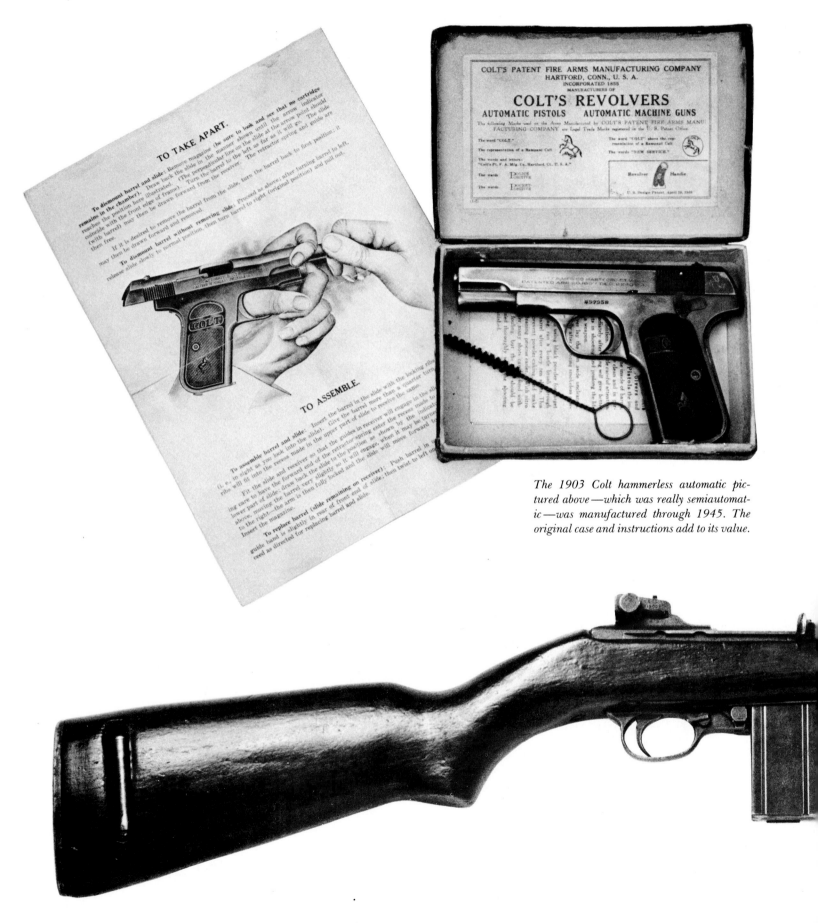

The 1903 Colt hammerless automatic pictured above—which was really semiautomatic—was manufactured through 1945. The original case and instructions add to its value.

Many 8-shot 9mm Walther P-38s like the one above were "liberated" by World War II GIs. The identical pistol remained in production in postwar West Germany, but World War II models can be identified by the last two numbers in the manufacturer's code: 43 marks a 1943 gun.

This M-1 carbine, issued to American troops in World War II, was manufactured by IBM, though eight other manufacturers also made the gun. The capacity of the magazine used determines whether the semiautomatic .30-caliber weapon fires 5, 15 or 30 cartridges before reloading.

When the ten barrels of the Gatling gun, one of the earliest machine guns, are rotated by a hand crank, the force of gravity drops cartridges into the chambers from a magazine (not shown) above them. A hinge across a yoke permits vertical aiming, and the yoke swivels sideways. This particular gun, made by Colt in 1897 and used in Cuba during the Spanish-American War, fired between 600 and 1,000 rounds per minute. Hanging between the wheels is a can of grease.

MUSEUMS
Colonial Williamsburg Foundation
Williamsburg, Virginia 23185

J. M. Davis Gun Museum
Claremore, Oklahoma 74017

Greenfield Village and Henry Ford Museum
Dearborn, Michigan 48121

National Museum of History and Technology
Smithsonian Institution
Washington, D.C. 20560

Springfield Armory Museum
Springfield, Massachusetts 01103

Wadsworth Atheneum
Hartford, Connecticut 06103

War Memorial Museum of Virginia
Newport News, Virginia 23607

West Point Museum
West Point, New York 10996

The Winchester Gun Museum
The Buffalo Bill Historical Center
Cody, Wyoming 82414

COLLECTORS ORGANIZATIONS
National Rifle Association
1600 Rhode Island Avenue, N.W.
Washington, D.C. 20036

PERIODICALS
Arms Gazette, Beinfeld Publishing, Inc., North
Hollywood, California 91605

The Gun Report, World-Wide Gun Report, Inc.,
Aledo, Illinois 61231

BOOKS
Chapel, Charles Edward, *The Complete Book of Gun
Collecting.* Coward-McCann, Inc., 1960.

Flayderman, Norm, *Flayderman's Guide to Antique
American Firearms.* Follett Publishing Company, 1977.

Lindsay, Merrill:
The Lure of Antique Arms. David McKay Company, Inc.,
1976.
One Hundred Great Guns. Walker & Co., 1967.

Moore, Warren, *Weapons of the American Revolution
. . . and Accoutrements.* Funk & Wagnalls, 1967.

Peterson, Harold L., and Robert Elman, *The Great
Guns.* Grosset & Dunlap, Inc., 1971.

Wilkinson, Frederick, *Antique Guns and Gun
Collecting.* Hamlyn, 1974.

Handbags
Purses to Treasure

A tiny party bag of the 1920s is made of silk covered with tinted ostrich feathers. The purse could hold little more than a compact.

In June 1978, at an auction of Americana in Massachusetts, seven small handbags—needlework purses and pocketbooks—dating from the 18th and early 19th Centuries were sold for $1,100. Some of these purses measured only a few inches across. The price paid for them is an indication of the rarity of early American handbags. Fortunately for collectors, however, the prices paid for some of the more common handbags, while increasing, have not yet soared into the four-figure range. In fact, in 1978 I generally spent no more than $40 on an average purchase, and I was frequently able to buy bags for as little as five dollars.

Collectors classify handbags of any period under a number of categories: the kind of construction employed, such as beading, embroidery or other kinds of

Robert Pusilo is a costume designer for movies and television. Since the early 1960s he has collected several hundred handbags, a number of which date from the 17th Century.

needlework; the materials used—whether fabric, metal or leather—and the style of design.

The most common type of construction a beginning collector is likely to encounter is beaded work. Beaded handbags are exceedingly durable because beads cover the outside completely, forming a protective layer over threads and fabric. Before the 1850s the beads used were glass and were smaller and more intense in color than those that followed. Cut-steel beads became popular around the 1840s and continued to show up, with glass beads, in handbags made as late as the 1930s. As it happens, it was with beaded bags of the 1920s that I started collecting.

One day, at a time when I was designing Victorian-style costumes, I looked over handbags I had bought earlier, thinking they were all from the 1920s. I came across one *(page 101)* with tiny, tightly knit beads and a design divided into horizontal panels. The colors, to put

it mildly, were quite distinctive—electric blue and brick red. From my studies of clothing styles, I realized suddenly that this purse was at least 70 years older than I had thought. It had to have been made between the late 1830s and the early 1850s, when such designs commonly appeared in handbags. This discovery spurred me to search for at least one good example of a handbag from every decade from the 1850s to the 1920s. I did much better than I had hoped: my collection now goes back to 1650.

As often seen in most collections as beaded bags are examples of embroidery construction. Among my favorites is a simple linen purse *(page 104)*. I picked it up several years ago at a Pennsylvania flea market for $10.

A knowledge of fabrics can help date a bag. It takes experience to tell the difference between, say, early-, mid- and late-19th Century silks, but other materials are easy to distinguish, and their popularity varied from period to period. Linen, for example, had its heyday in the early part of the 19th Century, and plush had its day later on, during the 1880s.

Leather on metal frames became a major competitor of various fabrics in the making of handbags from about the 1880s. Many leather bags were fitted with compartments that fulfilled special functions: an opera bag held opera glasses, for example, as well as a powder puff. Surprisingly, old leather handbags are often the hardest to find, although not necessarily the most expensive; they were used every day until they wore out, and then were thrown away.

Hardier than leather bags were those made of metal. Bagmakers started constructing woven-mesh purses as early as the 1820s; chain-link mesh, used in the 1890s, had increased in popularity by the 1920s and is still be-

The handwork on this French drawstring bag is representative of the period from the late 1830s to the early 1850s. The gazebo shown in the design is a needlewoman's tour de force.

ing manufactured today. Those handbags of the 1920s can easily be found in flea markets, but they have risen steeply in price because they have become chic as evening accessories.

The style as well as the material of a bag can be a clue to dating it. A typical bag of the 1920s is small, flat and rectangular in shape, and often the mesh is enameled *(page 109);* Egyptian motifs, geometric designs and embroidered leather are other characteristics commonly seen during this period. Among older bags are the long, tubular ones known as stocking, or miser's, purses *(page 103)* carried by both men and women from the late 18th Century until about 1880; they apparently originated with the medieval practice of carrying coins in the toe of a stocking. In the first quarter of the 19th Century small drawstring purses, known as reticules, predominated. Around the 1860s they were superseded by flat, squarish pocketbooks, and from the 1870s onward by triangularly shaped clasp bags. Victorian and Edwardian women wore purses that fastened to a belt, often with a large ornamental clasp.

When I purchase a vintage handbag, I always check to see that it has no holes, is not faded and has its beading or embroidery intact. I avoid leather that is brittle and silk that is splitting. Naturally, it is more desirable to acquire a bag that still has all its original parts, such as a carrying chain and lining, but very often some worn part has been replaced. For example, when beaded dresses and handbags became the rage in the 1920s, many beaded bags of an earlier vintage were brought out of storage and their original, frayed drawstring tops were replaced. Unlike some collectors, I have no objection to alterations provided they are skillfully done and are not passed off as original.

I am willing to do a certain amount of restoration myself, such as repairing minor damage to needlework and beadwork. Knitted and crocheted beadwork, however, is very difficult to restore. Careful cleaning can work wonders. I apply reconditioning cream to leather and gently suds any light-colored washable items in mild soap and distilled water.

I have found handbags of all ages everywhere from flea markets and antique shows to junk shops and charity stores. I also buy bags through the mail from dealers who acquire merchandise at estate sales. Some collectors prefer antique shops and seek out old handbags bearing the labels of such well-known designers as Joseph of Paris. I prefer the hustle and bustle of a busy flea market. I would far rather discover a handmade bag signed and dated by an American woman who had fashioned it with her own hands.

For related material, see the article on Embroidery in a separate volume of this encyclopedia.

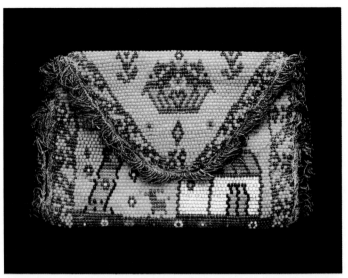

A rare French beaded bag of the 18th Century has a gilt fringe and an unusual design of geometric figures and, below the flap, a farmhouse.

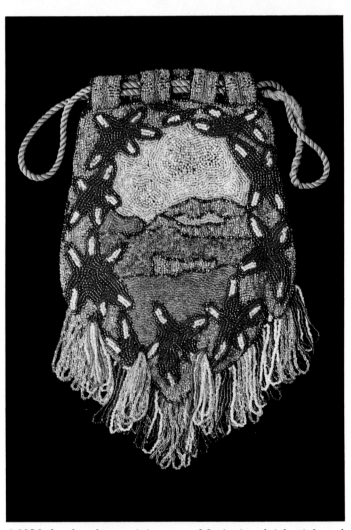

A 1920s bag has characteristics unusual for its time: bright pinks and greens, fringe sprouting from the design, and raised beadwork.

Glass beads and a length of 7 inches date this compartmentalized stocking purse to the 1840s. Two small rings slide to close the opening in the center that provides access to each of the end compartments. A larger purse was used in the 18th and early 19th Centuries.

This 1910 beaded bag with a clasp that can expand is relatively common. The ring on the chain could be used to attach the bag to a belt.

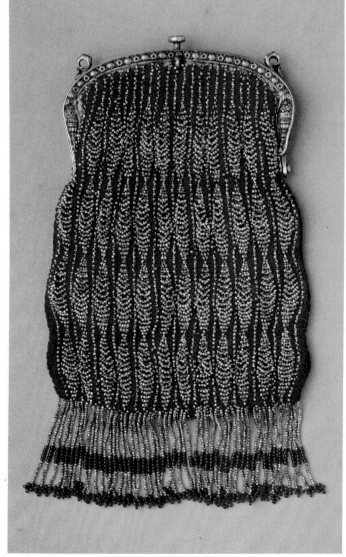

Unusual decorative treatment for a 1920s bag is the raised beadwork—in crimson glass and silvery cut steel—that cascades from the frame.

The drawstring purse above was made around 1650, probably in England. It is 5 inches wide; the embroidery was worked with silk thread.

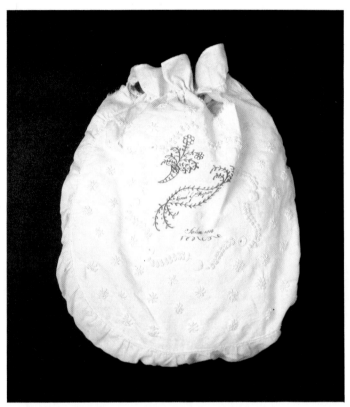

Signed with the owner's name, Sarah G. Ingres, and marked "Salem 1818," this reticule is embroidered linen decorated with ink.

Its triangular shape, dark velvet and heavy ajour, or openwork, frame date this purse to the 1870s. It is embroidered with metallic thread.

Made in Europe between 1840 and 1860, a canvas bag exhibits well-preserved, well-executed petit-point embroidery and tassels of chenille.

Above is a bag from the 1820s, reproduced in actual size. The floral design is executed in bright colors on dark silk in the kind of embroidery known as tambour work.

The three drawstring bags above date from the mid-19th Century. The two at top are of knitted and crocheted silk with sectioned designs; the other is of knitted and pleated cotton in the popular Zouave design, imitating the silk sashes of Algerian soldiers of the period.

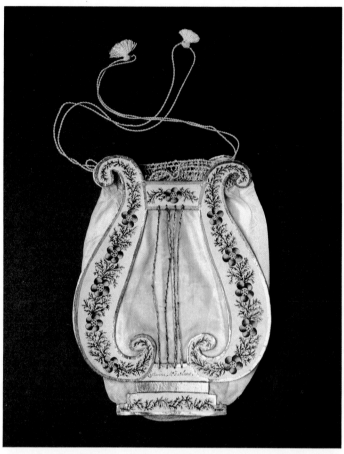

An early-19th Century silk drawstring bag is decorated with a gold-edged lyre made of well-preserved paper, which is rarely found.

This betasseled French purse—2 ¼ inches wide, just large enough for a coin or two—was made in the 1860s of silk woven with metallic threads.

A 1920s purse of woven silk has its florid design carried out even on the strap. The red Celluloid clasp, like the design, is Art Deco in style.

A leather bag 6 inches wide, probably made in the late 19th Century, has sides of woven straw that have survived in remarkably good condition.

Vintage leather handbags are scarce today. The stamped one above, with machine stitching and a snap clasp, dates from the turn of the century.

A small handbag of the 1860s is made of velvet plush appliquéd with leather; it has cut-steel and bead decorations.

Made of fine, woven mesh with a paper lining, this bag of the 1820s or 1830s, 3 inches wide, was meant to be worn on a belt at the waist.

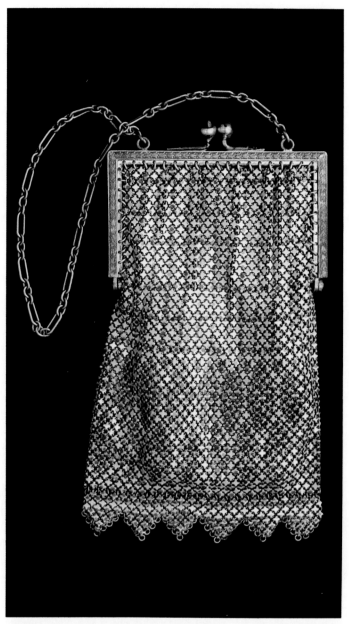

A 1920s enameled-mesh bag has a jagged bottom edge in the style called dagging, a decorative device that originated in the 14th Century.

The mesh of a French purse made about 1850 resembles fine window screening. The chainlike outline in the frame is of braided cut beads.

COLLECTORS ORGANIZATIONS
The Costume Society of America
c/o The Costume Institute
The Metropolitan Museum of Art
New York, New York 10028

BOOKS
Buck, Anne M., *Victorian Costume and Costume Accessories*. Universe Books, 1970.

Hatpins
Fancy Anchors for Fancy Headgear

The collector arranges a glittering assortment of glass-headed hatpins in a pitcher to make a grouping for display.

I n 1913 and 1914, even as World War I bore down upon Europe, a battle was being waged against hatpins. Women's hats had been growing steadily in size and had by this time become gigantic. To skewer the hats in place on top of towering hair, women were using pins as long as 14 inches. Two or three such pins jabbed through a hat with the points protruding made a woman a walking barb.

In Europe and America an enraged outcry went up from punctured males. News reports and letters to the editor lashed out against "unprotected hatpins . . . which endanger life and limb." One man sustained a "deep and painful cut" riding an elevated train in Brooklyn; it led to blood poisoning, large doctor's bills, a permanent scar, two weeks away from work—a heavy burden for "a young fellow with a mother dependent on him." Some cities banned unshielded hatpins, and some bellicose women received police sum-

Lillian Baker is the founder of an organization for hatpin and hatpin-holder collectors and author of a book on the subjects.

monses for defying the law. Partly because of the outcry but probably more because hat styles shrank, manufacture of hatpins more than 9 inches long did not last. As a result, long hatpins are hard to find today and are much in demand by collectors.

In addition to the long, potentially lethal hatpins, collectors look for decorative examples made from about 1850 to about 1925. The most valuable bear the marks of designers known for creations other than hatpins: America's Louis Comfort Tiffany, noted for his art glass

Enlarged to twice their actual size are four hatpins with floral designs in the Art Nouveau style of the Edwardian period, when the most elaborate hats—and hatpins—were in vogue. Two are gilded brass, one is oxidized nickel silver (second from left) and the other sterling.

and lamps; France's René Lalique, famed for glasswork; Russia's Peter Carl Fabergé, creator of jeweled Easter eggs for the czar; and Denmark's Georg Jensen, designer of silverware. Most of their hatpins are marked on the reverse of the hatpin head or along the pin shaft: Tiffany's "LCT," Lalique's "R. Lalique" or "R. L.," and Jensen's "Jensen" or "G. J." Some Fabergé hatpins are unmarked, but others bear "Fabergé" in Roman or Russian Cyrillic letters, while still others have the initials of the craftsman.

Almost as desirable as the hatpins by noted artists, but less costly, are those made by notable jewelers and silversmiths: in America, Gorham Manufacturing Co. (marked "Martelé" or "Athenic"), Unger Bros. (an intersecting "UB") and Tiffany & Co. (the company name); in England, Charles Horner, Ltd. ("CH").

A special category is vanities, hatpins serving a dual purpose. I have found compacts, perfume vials, pin holders, even a detachable top to be worn as a brooch.

Because of increasing interest in hatpins, fakes have been made. Many are 9- or 12-inch steel shanks soldered to old buttons or fobs. I look for soldering and check that the metal of the shank suits that of the ornament— gold heads usually had gilded shanks. If a shank bends easily, it could never have been pushed through a hat, so a flexible shank usually indicates a fake.

Many fine hatpins have been cannibalized to be made into jewelry. I rescued one of my prizes, a foxhead pin *(page 114)* from this fate. I had been eyeing it at an antique show when I learned that a man had already bought the pin and—to my consternation—pulled the head off for a ring. Fortunately I was able to persuade him to let me buy it from him, and I put it back together.

For related material, see the article on Hats in this volume, and the articles on Buttons and Jewelry in separate volumes of The Encyclopedia of Collectibles.

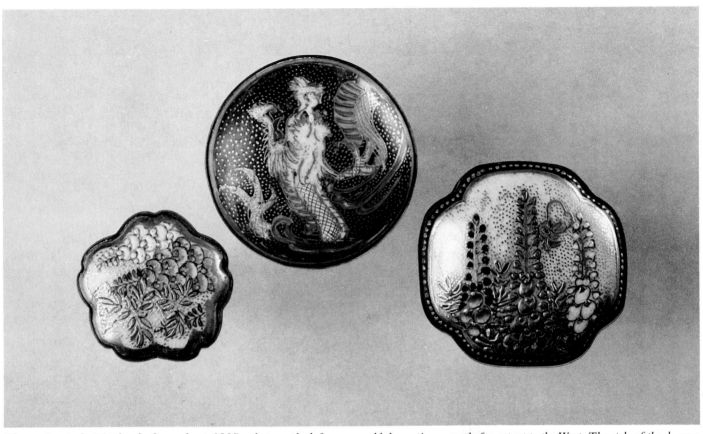

These ceramic hatpin heads from about 1885, photographed from above, are Satsuma ware—a crackle-glazed Japanese porcelain with gold decoration—made for export to the West. The style of the dragon and flowers is characteristic of Satsuma pottery.

The mosaic hatpins below, fashioned of tiny pieces of colored glass, were probably made between 1850 and 1870. The cube, ⅜ inch on each side, has 6 floral designs, the ball 12.

The workmanship of this unmarked hatpin —red enamel with gold, pearls and yellow quartz—suggests it came from Russian jeweler Peter Carl Fabergé around 1870.

Enameled by a technique called plique-à-jour, which creates a stained-glass effect, a French hatpin from around 1910 is accented with steely-looking marcasites and green quartz.

A stylized design of molded leaves and vines is overlaid with gold in a Bohemian-glass pin, shown above in a top view hiding the shank. The collector bought it for $30 in 1974.

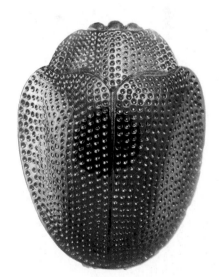

This scarab pin is of carnival glass, the inexpensive material used for giveaways during the 1920s. At that time a vogue for Egyptian styles made scarab designs popular.

Hatpins of faceted glass, like the five reproduced at left, were inexpensive when they were made and remain inexpensive today, especially the smaller ones. They were particularly popular at the beginning of the 20th Century.

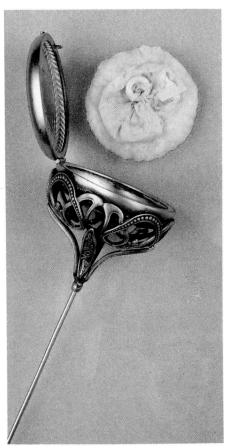

A gold fox-head ornament with eyes made of diamonds tops the hatpin above. The ornament measures ¾ inch in width.

Above is a pair of silver hatpins depicting Hiawatha and his bride in a holder embossed with a stanza from Henry Wadsworth Longfellow's poem "The Song of Hiawatha."

A prized brass hatpin (above) conceals a compact with powder puff and a mirror. It is unusually large—2 inches across.

Made of sterling silver with blue brilliants, this hatpin has a sought-after Art Nouveau motif—a woman's head with flowing locks.

Two of these hatpins—the ones at left and third from left—are fakes, made with a fob and a button. They lack the small metal tube, a type of jeweler's findings, that in the genuine pins connects the head to the shank.

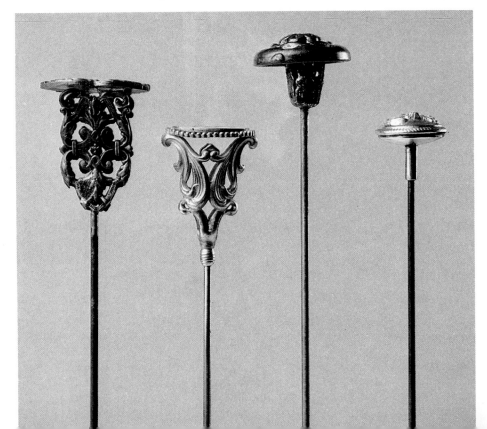

Holders for Pins

Hatpin holders, many made like vases with perforated tops, provide authentic, attractive storage and display for hatpins. They were produced of every grade of pottery as well as glass, metal, fabric and straw, and are still common. Many collectors consider European ones the most attractive. Desirable German porcelain holders bear such marks as "R S Prussia," "Royal Bayreuth," "Royal Rudolstadt," "Rosenthal" and "R S Germany." Royal Doulton of England and the porcelain factories in Limoges, France, also made valuable holders. Less expensive are Japanese imports. Those made before 1921 are marked "Nippon"; later ones, "Made in Japan."

Some reproductions are being sold as originals. Collectors should be wary of hand-painted porcelain holders with a concave top and a small saucer attached. Some are unmarked, some bear the mark "R S Prussia" on the base. If they have no overglaze they are probably fakes.

Ceramic sugar shakers are sometimes mistaken for hatpin holders. The shakers are usually plumper than hatpin holders and have fewer holes in the top and, of course, a round hole in the base through which they are filled.

This hatpin holder of the unglazed porcelain called bisque, molded in the shape of an Oriental woman, was made by a German firm.

A cameo decorates an elegant and unusual holder designed to hang on a wall. It was manufactured in Germany around 1895.

Two hand-painted holders bear marks on the bases: "Rosenthal" from Germany (left) and "W. A. Picard—N & Co.—France."

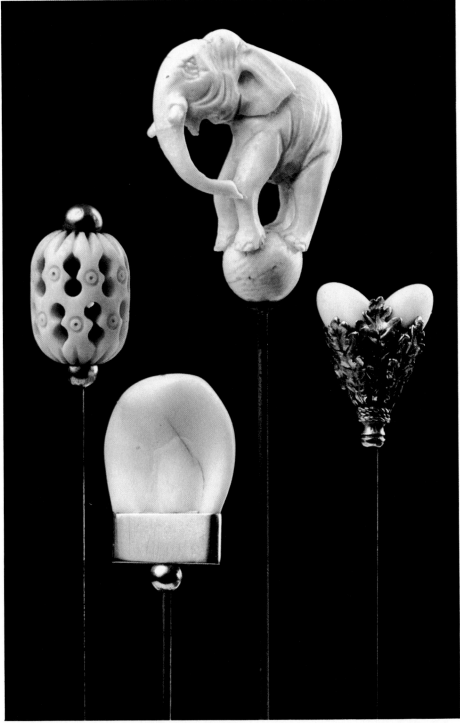

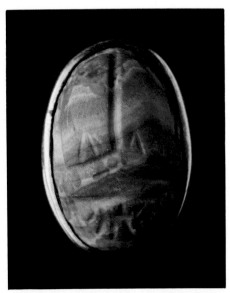

The Egyptian scarab above was carved from malachite, a copper mineral, thousands of years ago; it was mounted in sterling to serve as the head of a hatpin in the 1920s.

The four hatpins above are all fashioned from natural materials. From the left they are carved bone, a tooth (probably from an elk) mounted in gold, carved ivory, and two small deer teeth in a silver setting. The most valuable of the four is the ivory-elephant hatpin.

At right is a ½-inch-wide hatpin with an unfaceted amethyst that is set in an ornate Victorian mounting. The pin shank, part of which is visible, is 5 ½ inches long.

These six hatpins from about 1910 are unusual for their distinctive mineral ornaments. From the left they are polished amber, rough ame- *thyst crystals, polished malachite, moonstone in a monogrammed silver mount, lapis lazuli, and fool's gold, or shiny iron pyrite, in a wire mount.*

COLLECTORS ORGANIZATIONS
International Club for
Collectors of Hatpins and
Hatpin Holders
15237 Chanera Avenue
Gardena, California 90249

BOOKS
Baker, Lillian, *The Collector's Encyclopedia of Hatpins and Hatpin Holders.* Collector Books, 1976.

Meyer, Florence E., *Pins for Hats and Cravats Worn by Ladies and Gentlemen.* Wallace-Homestead Book Co., 1974.

Hats
Collecting Yesterday's Chic

In the late 1930s Elsa Schiaparelli, the Paris designer who was famous for sometimes bizarre innovations—one was a color she called shocking pink—introduced a hat that looked like an outsized cocktail slipper upside down. It was to be worn with the high heel sticking up from the back of the head. Around the same time a New York designer named Germaine Vittu offered a hat that resembled a head of Bibb lettuce. Neither the cocktail slipper nor the lettuce hat won general acceptance when it first appeared, but both fascinate me as a collector of headgear because they are so outlandish—and characteristic not only of hats in the 1930s but also

Jimaxi Ostrowski became a collector of hats after she studied 19th Century millinery in books and museums in order to recreate a bonnet of the Civil War era for a local pageant.

of my favorite styles, the millinery worn during the Edwardian era. At that time artificial vegetation and feathers enveloped hats; by 1911 some measured as much as 2 yards around the brim.

Though my taste focuses on that elegant time before World War I, I gladly include older hats, the older the better. Those made before 1800 are very scarce and most collectors, myself included, concentrate on the periods following. In the early 19th Century, the dominant style for women was the bonnet—defined as anything worn on the head that fitted closely and tied under the chin. Considered proper for most occasions, bonnets were made in a number of variations. Among the best-known bonnet styles was the poke, which got its name from the way the brim reached out from the face. Over the decades, the bonnet shrank and lost its chin ties until by the 1870s the fashionable headgear could no longer be called a bonnet; it was a small hat.

The alert observer of couture could have predicted that the small hat-bonnet of the late Victorians would blossom into Edwardian extravagance and then shrink again. Just as hats were achieving their widest Edwardian expanse a head-hugging, almost brimless style ap-

Cloth roses and stock blossoms cover the crown of a straw hat from about 1910, when women's headgear stretched to landscape-blocking dimensions. Their extravagant size and adornment make them prizes today.

peared. A well-known example was the cloche, the most popular hat shape of the 1920s *(page 127)*. These hats, along with a few from the 1930s and 1940s, seem to be the most recent to attract the attention of collectors—in the decades following, the dress-up hat practically disappeared from fashionable wardrobes.

Men's fashions do not undergo changes as dramatic—or interesting—as women's, and male headgear forms only a small part of my collection. However, certain classic shapes such as the boater *(page 127)* and topper *(pages 121 and 122)* are particularly interesting. The topper is noteworthy because in the early 19th Century it was made of beaver fur that had been felted—subjected to heat, moisture and pressure to mat and smooth the fibers into a glossy, water-repellent material. So great was the demand for beaver during the height of this fashion that vast stretches of North America were explored for the first time primarily to find trapping grounds where beavers had not yet become scarce.

Beaver hats were understandably expensive, but old ones are not unreasonably costly today. The topper on page 122 cost $25 in 1975, which makes it an expensive purchase. The most I have paid for a hat was $30, for the calash on page 120. The least was 10 cents, for a feathered toque, a small brimless woman's hat.

Fortunately, such prices do not make it worthwhile to fake a collectible hat, and I do not worry about deliberate frauds. I do keep an eye open for theatrical reproductions, though, because they occasionally find their way into flea markets and antique shops, generally betraying their lack of age by the newness of their materials. For example, straw in old hats is usually brittle, while in a theatrical reproduction it is likely to be quite supple.

While on guard for the occasional reproduction, I have been lucky in my searches and have found hats in such unpredictable places as a counter selling carpenters' tools. Good places to look for hats also include estate auctions, where I recommend looking in closets.

Once acquired, collectible hats are strictly not for wearing—by you or anyone else—if they are to retain their value. A friend of mine once lent a collapsible silk opera hat from the 1940s to a local theater group for a performance. Since then, he has been the owner of a permanently collapsed hat.

A curved frame of reed or wire, over which fabric was gathered, shaped so-called reed bonnets like this one, a style popular in the mid-1800s.

This 18th Century forerunner of the Victorian bonnet was called a calash because, like the carriage of that name, it had a folding top. The calash was a popular style, and many examples have survived.

The silk-lined straw bonnet above is unusual because it is so well preserved even though it is more than 100 years old.

The poke bonnet, the brim of which poked out, was a popular style during the early-Victorian era. The one above is silk brocade.

An 1840s top hat—a rare find—is made of felted wool rather than the beaver fur then so prized (page 122). Light colors like fawn, dove gray and white were popular when this one was made.

Many 1850s bonnets were trimmed inside and out like this one, combining maple leaves, forget-me-nots, lace, and black and white ribbons.

In the 1860s some bonnets had brims that peaked above the forehead. The example at right is edged with pillow, or bobbin, lace made by twisting threads wound on bobbins.

An 1860s stovepipe hat has straight sides, unlike the curved topper that preceded it (page 121). This example is of costly felt made from beaver fur—glossy and water resistant.

During the 1870s the style rather fancifully called shepherdess, popular a century earlier, was revived. Shown in a hand-crocheted silk version, the hat was worn tipped forward as if slipping off a high-piled hairdo.

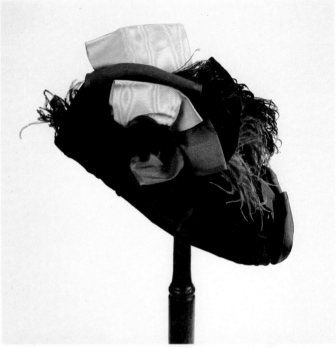

This hat from the 1870s, part of a bride's trousseau, was included in a trunk full of old clothes found in a barn. It is made of velvet and trimmed with ostrich-feather tips and silk and velvet ribbons.

By the 1870s the distinction between bonnets, which tied under the chin, and hats, which sat unsecured on the head, was blurred by creations like the straw above; it could be worn either way.

Hats with high crowns, the height of fashion for a few years in the 1880s, are rarely found in good condition because the crowns are easily crushed. The collector had to repair this one.

A stuffed bird of paradise swoops down the side of an 1880s straw—a particularly rare find because bird trimming almost never survives intact.

Roses and a spray of wheat stalks top a thickly woven straw hat from the 1890s, which still bears its original Paris label.

The straw Panama for men—named for the country where the hats were first marketed—became popular in the 1890s. The best were so finely braided that they resembled linen.

The crown of an early-20th Century velvet hat is completely buried in a mass of dyed ostrich feathers. The popularity of the feathers led to the establishment of ostrich farms to supply milliners.

The simple helmet shape above was first announced as the "new bonnet" in 1910, just when hats were reaching their most extravagant size. It presaged the very popular cloche of the 1920s (right).

A swirl of feathers surrounds a 1920s hat originally worn with a mourning costume. These feathers came from egrets, but milliners—ill-versed in ornithology—commonly misidentified them as osprey feathers.

The Eugénie hat of 1931 was a revival of a style originally called the Empress—after the French Empress Eugénie—when it was first popular in 1859. The one above is felt trimmed with an ostrich plume.

The stiff straw boater, first worn by English oarsmen, became fashionable summer wear for men from the 1880s to the 1940s.

Cloches with minimal adornment (like the straw at left above) became the predominant women's style during the '20s.

This style of plain felt hat—it was made without a crown but with a large brim—was briefly fashionable for late-afternoon wear during the 1950s.

Adapted from the traditional sailor's cap, a 1940s stitched felt hat twists to a peak. It was worn rakishly tilted forward and slightly askew.

A jaunty 1940s hat combines two colors and two weaves in straw, with a starched and painted feather that probably once belonged to a pheasant.

MUSEUMS
The Millinery Shop
Colonial Williamsburg, Virginia 23185

Patti McClain's Museum of Vintage Fashion
Dunsmuir House and Gardens
Oakland, California 94605

COLLECTORS ORGANIZATIONS
The Costume Society of America
c/o The Costume Institute
The Metropolitan Museum of Art
New York, New York 10028

BOOKS
Blum, Stella, ed., *Victorian Fashions and Costumes from Harper's Bazar 1867-1898.* Dover Publications, Inc., 1974.

Buck, Anne, *Victorian Costume and Costume Accessories.* Universe Books, 1970.

de Courtais, Georgine, *Women's Headdress and Hairstyles in England from AD 600 to the Present Day.* B. T. Batsford, Ltd., 1973.

Wilcox, R. Turner, *The Mode in Hats and Headdress.* Charles Scribner's Sons, 1945.

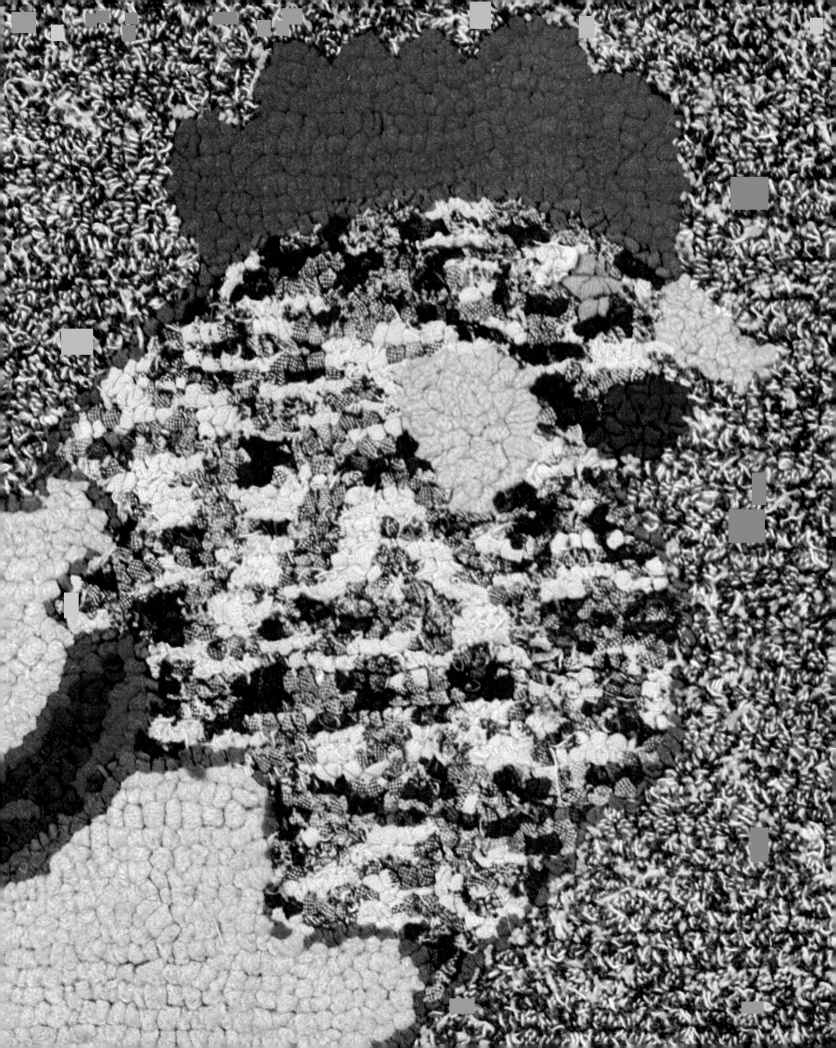

Hooked Rugs
Homespun Designs for the Floor

The collectors of hooked rugs quickly discover that many of these prized antiques exhibit a striking similarity in design—unusual in things individually handmade at home by many thousands of women. The explanation is simple. By the 1870s, many rug hookers were using printed patterns.

The earliest rugs followed hand-drawn, personally created designs. But in 1868 a Maine peddler named Edward Sands Frost, while helping his wife work on a

---

In 1972, Ilon Specht Case, an advertising executive, and Dalmar Tifft, an interior designer, began collecting hooked rugs as a joint hobby.

---

rug a cousin had drawn for her, decided he could do better himself. He made sheet-metal stencils for leaves, flowers, scrolls and animals, then combined them for different patterns. Altogether he made about 750 stencils, with which 180 patterns could be created.

Frost, who had taken up peddling as a healthful outdoor occupation a few years before on his doctor's advice, hawked his patterns to delighted customers along

The detail at left of a 20th Century hooked rug —the full 46-by-37-inch rug is above —reveals loops of yarn, hooked through a ground fabric, that create the design. This rug was probably made after 1920; the tweedy background and the colors seldom were used before then.

his rural route. He retired to California in 1876, selling his lucrative business to James A. Strout, who carried on until 1900. Some of his patterns also were copied by another late-19th Century firm of rug-pattern sellers, E. Ross & Company, of Toledo, Ohio, and presumably by others. Without a doubt many rug hookers also copied by hand from a neighbor's ready-made design.

The rugs, graced with lions, palms and many other designs, were simple to make. Loops of material—yarn or wool rags cut into strips—were hooked through the interstices of a coarsely woven ground fabric to form a pile. Unlike the loops in other pile rugs, those in hooked rugs were not knotted *(page 135)*.

Although rugs have been hooked in many countries, they were most popular in America. Early American hooked rugs, made before 1850, were done on a linen ground. They are hard to find now. Most post-1850s rugs were done on burlap, an inexpensive material made from jute and sold by many dry-goods stores and mail-order houses; jute also was made into feed sacks, which when empty became grounds for rugs. These sacks, about 46 by 40 inches with the seams opened, explain the shape and size of many rugs. Square rugs used the entire opened sack, while rectangular ones used one side only. Fewer semicircular, round or oval rugs were made, perhaps because these shapes wasted burlap.

Collectors began to buy hooked rugs in the 1920s and 1930s, and they cleaned out most back-country attics and barns. Today, collectors face an arduous hunt. Folk-art dealers usually have a few rugs at any given time. But many found in flea markets or antique shops are faded, ragged and small; they are often of fairly recent date.

Design and condition outweigh other factors in value, such as age or size. Age is hard to determine except in a very general way—early 20th Century (meaning 1900 to 1930) or 19th Century is the dating usually given even by prestigious auction houses. A date hooked into the rug itself is no evidence of age: it might have been put there only to commemorate a historical event that took place long before the rug was hooked.

Among designs, the so-called pictorial type is more desirable than floral and geometric patterns. Pictorial rugs show people, animals, ships, houses and landscapes, or commemorate personal or historical events.

A mid-19th Century rug depicts not only a man and a woman wearing a kerchief, each carrying a gun, but also dogs, an owl, a red-breasted robin and trees. The unique pictorial imagery and the size —88 by 42 inches, unusually large for an old rug—make this specimen very valuable.

A pictorial rug, hooked with wool strips on a burlap ground in the late 19th Century, is unusual because of its shape—it was made to be a doormat.

People and landscapes are scarcest, while animals—especially dogs, cats and horses—are fairly numerous. At a 1978 auction of American antiques, a 1920s rug 45 by 33 inches, showing a ship and its name, brought $500. A similar rug of the same size, showing a man, a woman, a ship and a six-line inscription, sold for $750.

Floral designs are common. Sometimes the flowers are fairly realistic, as in the rug shown at the top of page 142. Others are stylized, like the one on page 143, approaching the geometrics in effect.

All three design types are found in rugs made on printed as well as hand-drawn patterns. Hand-drawn designs, especially the unique ones made by or for rug hookers, are naturally valued more. They were used even after the Maine peddler introduced printed patterns. The popularity of ready-mades is seen in the 1895 Montgomery Ward & Co. catalogue, offering 15 different patterns at 23 to 60 cents each: flowers, cats, two "Turkish," or "Oriental," styles, a lion with palm trees and a "large, intelligent-looking dog lying on a lawn, lake and mountain in the distance. Grecian border."

It is generally possible to recognize these commercial-pattern rugs because the same patterns were used for so many rugs. While they are generally valued less than those with hand-drawn designs, some are worth more than others. The least desirable betray their origin by their exact symmetry, sameness of repeated motifs, or absence of any odd or idiosyncratic symbols. More valuable than a rug made with absolute fidelity to the pattern is one in which the maker's individuality overcame or obscured the perfection of the store-bought design.

Regardless of the origin of the pattern, a rug should be in fairly good condition to be worth buying. If it sheds fine tan dust, the ground fabric is probably disintegrating. Nothing can be done about such deterioration, but most other defects, such as tears and bald spots, can be repaired if you use materials similar in texture and color to the original. Hooked rugs in good condition should be cleaned if dirty, but not in a washing machine or a dry-cleaning machine. The best way to clean a rug is to use a commercial rug cleaner with a sawdust or clay base, following instructions on the label.

Many collectors use their hooked rugs for their original purpose—to cover part of a floor. They are durable if you keep a felt pad underneath so that dirt will pass through the rug into the pad instead of grinding the rug against the bare floor. To store a rug, roll it with the pile out. Never keep a rug in a damp basement or a hot attic.

Sometimes you can rescue a rug from someone who does not appreciate it. We got one of our favorites—a floral from about 1890—this way. We bought a small painted chest at a country shop, then were amazed to see the dealer wrap it in a rug. When we offered to pay for the rug, she reluctantly took a dollar, saying it was really "no account." In fact, it was worth as much as the chest.

For related material, see the articles on Embroidery, Oriental Rugs and Quilts in other volumes of this encyclopedia.

This depiction of a dog and flowers is especially desirable for its pile. The loops of yarn for the dog were made high and then clipped, or sculpted, to vary from ½ to 2 ¼ inches. The sculpted effect is also called hoved up (see box below).

How a Rug Is Hooked

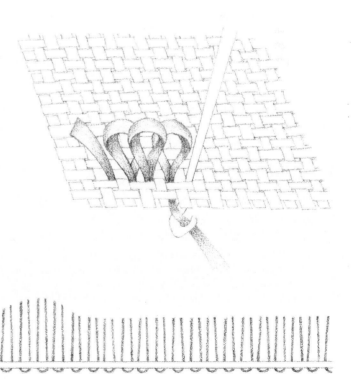

Hooked rugs are made with loops of yarn, strips of fabric or ribbon pulled through coarse ground fabric with a hook like that used for crocheting *(right)*. The loops, unknotted and unsewn, are secured only by the pressure of one against another; the more loops per square inch, the tighter the grip and more durable the rug. The finest rug may have 120 loops per square inch.

Below are three surface-finishing techniques. At left loops are even and unclipped, the most common finish. At right they are clipped straight. In the center is a three-dimensional sculpted variation sometimes called Waldoboro (after a Maine town where it was done) or hoved up.

UNCLIPPED LOOPS   **SCULPTED CLIPPING**   **STRAIGHT CLIPPING**

A unique rug that was made in the early 20th Century with a fine hooking technique and vibrant coloring has a motif unusual for this type of floor covering—a compass rose. The rose, like many, was designed in the shape of a star. The rug measures 35 inches on a side.

Like many other rug hookers, the maker of this one copied a popular quilt pattern—in this case one known as Log Cabin.

The pattern and the colors were popular during the late 19th Century and indicate that the rug was hooked then.

A geometric rug, hooked in yarn on burlap and left unclipped, bears a design called Broken Dish, one of several variations of patterns based on drawings made by tracing around pie plates or saucers. This rug was probably hooked between 1880 and 1900.

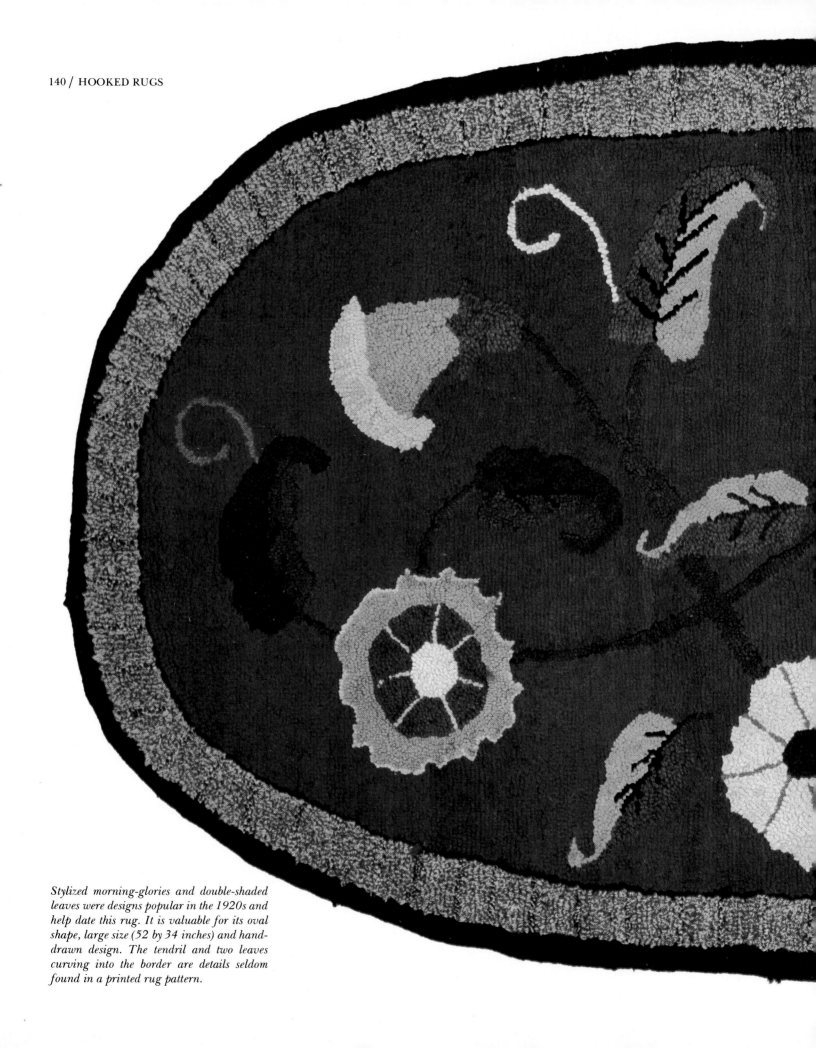

Stylized morning-glories and double-shaded leaves were designs popular in the 1920s and help date this rug. It is valuable for its oval shape, large size (52 by 34 inches) and hand-drawn design. The tendril and two leaves curving into the border are details seldom found in a printed rug pattern.

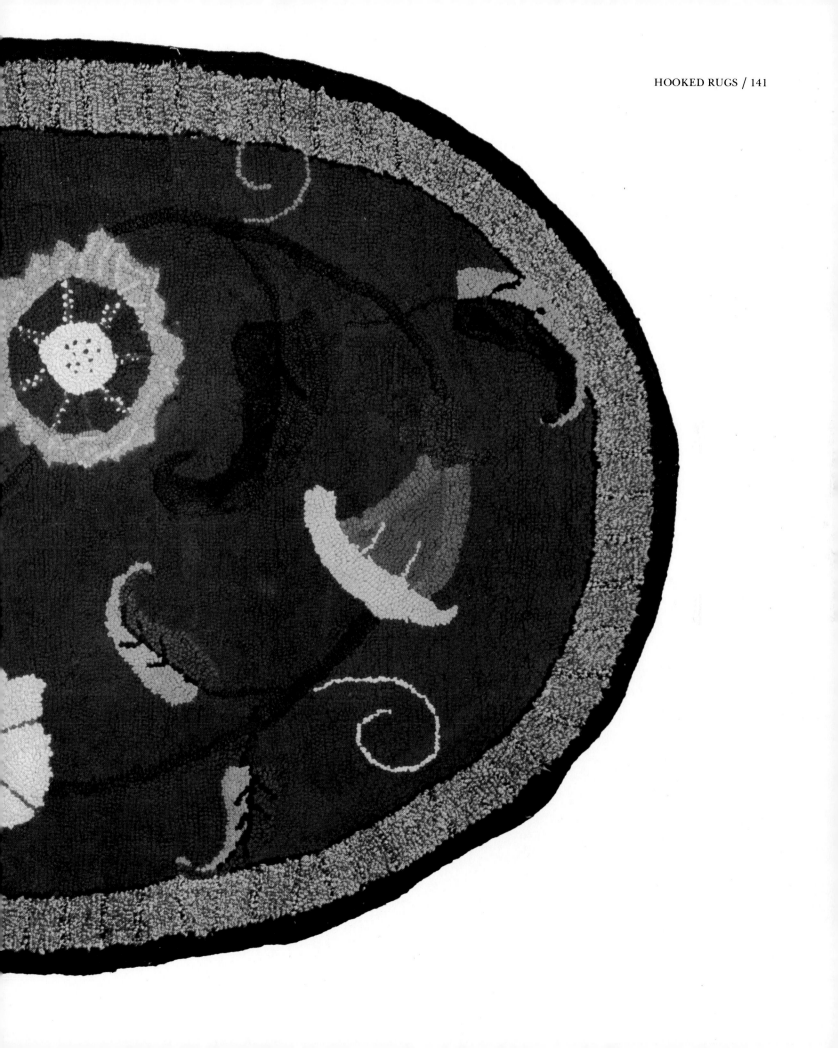

The floral rug above, made around 1850, is especially valuable for its color and the texture of its material, silk and wool-rag strips.

The shades of the blue, red and brown colors in this hooked rug from the 19th Century indicate that they were created by the use of vegetable dyes.

This rug was probably made in the 1920s —although similar stylized flowers were used earlier, the pale color in leaf veins and some diamonds was not.

MUSEUMS
The Currier Gallery of Art
Manchester, New Hampshire 03104

Greenfield Village and Henry Ford Museum
Dearborn, Michigan 48121

Henry Francis du Pont Winterthur Museum
Winterthur, Delaware 19735

Lincoln House, Old Sturbridge Village
Sturbridge, Massachusetts 01566

Museum of Early Southern Decorative Arts
Winston-Salem, North Carolina 27101

New Hampshire Historical Society
Concord, New Hampshire 03301

Shelburne Museum
Shelburne, Vermont 05482

BOOKS
Bowles, Ella Shannon, *Handmade Rugs.* Garden City
Publishing Company, Inc., 1937.

Edward Sands Frost's Hooked Rug Patterns. Greenfield

Village and Henry Ford Museum, 1970.

Kent, William Winthrop:
The Hooked Rug. Tower Books, 1971.
Rare Hooked Rugs. The Pond-Ekberg Company, 1948.

Kopp, Joel, and Kate Kopp:
American Hooked and Sewn Rugs, Folk Art Underfoot. E. P.
Dutton & Co., Inc., 1975.
Hooked Rugs in the Folk Art Tradition. Museum of
American Folk Art, 1974.

Little, Nina Fletcher, *Floor Coverings in New England
Before 1850.* Old Sturbridge Inc., 1972.

McGown, Pearl K., *The Dreams Beneath Design, A
Story of the History and Background of the
Designs of Hooked Rugs.* Bruce Humphries,
Inc., 1939.

Rex, Stella Hay, *Choice Hooked Rugs.* Prentice-Hall,
Inc., 1953.

Waugh, Elizabeth, and Edith Foley, *Collecting Hooked
Rugs.* The Century Co., 1927.

Horse-drawn Carriages
Relics of Old-Time Travel

My love for horse-drawn carriages goes back to the 1930s when my grandfather gave me a phaeton, a light, fast, four-wheeled vehicle named for the god of Greek mythology who dared to drive the chariot of the sun. As a young man I drove this smart rig the 75 miles between my family's Boston home and our summer place in Jaffrey, New Hampshire (the trip took two days), feeling like a god despite the jeers from passing motorists. In the years following, delight in horse-drawn vehicles led me

Horace K. Sowles Jr., a dealer in imported cars, has collected some 300 carriages since the 1930s. He is the secretary-treasurer of The Carriage Association of America, Inc., which has more than 2,000 members.

to collect several hundred of them, mostly American makes, ranging from swift two-wheeled gigs to hearses.

In the 1930s and 1940s, when almost nobody was interested in collecting carriages, I picked up some fine examples for less than $25. Hundreds of collectors have moved into the field in the intervening years, and in the '70s a few of my most valuable vehicles could command $25,000 each at auction. Driver-collectors in search of more affordable rigs often favor one-horse carriages such as the runabout at left or the sort of unadorned buggy that doctors once used; in 1978 small, easily maintained rigs of this kind could be bought in top condition for as little as $500, and might be knocked down to $50 if in need of restoration work.

Virtually all the carriages that survive in America date from 1800 to about 1910, when the motorcar began to take over private transportation. Before 1800 American roads were so few and so bad that people traveled on horseback, not in carriages, which would have shaken

The collector, wearing a boldly patterned "driving apron" to protect against dust, crosses a field near his Maine farm in a light carriage called a runabout. The vehicle, made about 1900 by Chauncey Thomas & Co., a leading Boston coachmaker, is natural-finish mahogany.

up their occupants unmercifully. Even towns that boasted cobblestone streets had few carriages until well after the Revolution because only the rich could afford them. As late as 1761 there were only 39 carriages in all of Philadelphia. However, as the 19th Century progressed, the nation's growing prosperity not only increased the numbers of citizens who could afford carriages but also paid for better roads.

All horse-drawn vehicles were made almost entirely of wood; metal, usually iron and steel, was used only for parts such as axles, tires, bolts, springs and suspension bars. The peak of carriage manufacture came during the mid-1870s, after mass-production methods were pioneered by carriage makers in Cincinnati. In 1900 no fewer than 907,483 pleasure carriages were manufactured in the United States in addition to thousands of farm carts, brewery wagons and other utilitarian vehicles. But 10 years later, the number of motorcars of all kinds that were made in this country came to 187,000, and horse-drawn carriages were on their way to becoming collectibles.

Collectors look for four basic types of carriage. Light vehicles for everyday use belong in the first group—two- or four-wheeled rigs that the owner drove himself, with room for two or three passengers. Owner-driven four-wheeled carriages that seated four or more people make up the second category. Collectible vehicles in the third group, notable for their elegance and designed to be driven by coachmen, came to be used as horse-drawn cabs. Commercial vehicles form the final category: carts and wagons used to transport goods and materials ranging from laundry to the bodies of the deceased. Sleighs are a highly collectible subcategory for those who live where the climate makes it possible to enjoy them as their makers intended.

No matter what their general preference among these categories, collectors tend to favor those carriages made by Brewster & Company of Connecticut and, later, New York. Three generations of the Brewster family ran the company, which was frequently called "the Tiffany of the carriage business," from the early 19th Century through 1927, when the last of the Brewsters retired. The founder was James Brewster, a perfectionist and an abstemious New England Puritan. He established the business in New Haven, Connecticut, in 1810. Prospering mightily from the sale of his vehicles, he planted 300 of New Haven's still-famous elm trees and ceaselessly delivered lectures to his hard-drinking me-

One of the earliest carriages built in America, a chaise (the French word for chair) was called a shay by some Americans. This one dates from 1790.

chanics on morals, religion and the evils of alcohol.

Brewster's two sons, Henry and James B., carried on his standards of excellent craftsmanship. Their carriages became bywords for solid workmanship, elegant design and sparkling paint-and-varnish finishes. Moving its headquarters to New York in 1856, the firm soon numbered among its faithful customers such men of legendary wealth as John Jacob Astor, J. Pierpont Morgan and Cornelius Vanderbilt. The Brewster brothers sent 13 carriages to the great Paris Exposition of 1878, where they won top honors over famous European manufacturers like Million Guiet of Paris and Hooper and Barker of London.

The last of the Brewsters, William (or Willie, as he was almost always called), grandson of the founder, personally inspected all carriages before they left the shop. If he noticed even the slightest imperfection in the varnished finish he whipped out a penknife and ripped a large X across the flawed panel, forcing the workmen to strip that piece down to the wood and do a complete refinishing job.

Brewster carriages were expensive when they were made—a Sears, Roebuck and Co. runabout cost as little as $21 in 1897, a similar Brewster rig cost $495 in 1901—and they remain costly. A fine Brewster phaeton, like the one pictured on page 151, would have been sold for $3,500, and a Brewster victoria—an open-air carriage that was named for the British monarch who favored them—for around $5,000 in 1975.

At such prices you should be sure that a carriage offered as a Brewster is authentic. Almost all carriage makers put their names on a small brass plate affixed to the back of the vehicle or—on a coach—on a brass plate inside the door. The Brewster name appears only on the hubcaps or oil caps. Unfortunately, even this identification is not a guarantee of authenticity; Brewster caps have been faked. A certain means of verification is the serial number that Brewster stamped on the seat under the cushion of each carriage. The same number is often recorded under the lamp mountings, on the axle and on the shafts. The Brewster serial number enables a buyer to ascertain who originally purchased the carriage: the firm maintained careful ledgers, listing each carriage's serial number, name of the purchaser, price and date.

These sales ledgers have survived over the years and are kept in the Manuscript Division of the New York Public Library and the New-York Historical Society. Should you discover a carriage bought by, say, Commodore Vanderbilt, you would be very fortunate. Vehicles that were once owned by famous people are particularly prized by collectors.

What Brewsters were to New York, Kimball carriages were to Chicago. C. B. Kimball, originally from Portland, Maine, opened his company in Chicago in 1877. A Kimball phaeton is highly desirable today. Firms that emulated the original James Brewster by making carriages in New Haven were G. & D. Cook and Henry Hooker & Co. The James Cunningham & Son Co. of Rochester, New York, specialized in lovely broughams driven by coachmen, which were enclosed, landaus, heavier than broughams and equipped with convertible tops, and hearses. The Thomas Goddard coachworks in Boston developed uniquely handy, four-wheeled buggies. Chauncey Thomas & Co., another top Boston firm, made a general line of vehicles, and Philadelphia prided itself on the elegant city vehicles of William D. Rogers. The leading maker of heavy working wagons in the country was Studebaker Brothers, of South Bend, Indiana, a name later famous in automobiles.

If he is extremely lucky, the beginning collector may still stumble across a fine carriage in an old barn. But a surer way to break into the field is to refer to *The Carriage Journal (page 160)*. Other sources include catalogues, price lists and notices of sales obtainable by writing to the Martin Auctioneers, Inc., of Blue Ball, Pennsylvania, specialists in horse-drawn vehicles, who hold three regular auctions each year: in May and August in Intercourse, Pennsylvania, a town located in the Amish country of the state, where people still use carriages for everyday transportation, and in July in East Springfield, Massachusetts.

Wherever the discovery turns up, the collector may find himself confronting a considerable repair job. For those who plan to do the work themselves, *The Carriage Journal,* which carried a readers' repair column for many years, should be a primary source of how-to information. Other 19th Century carriage-industry magazines are also helpful and interesting—not only in the practical business of repairs but also in the pursuit of carriage lore. The *New York Coach-Maker's Magazine,* founded in 1858 and absorbed into *The Hub* magazine in 1871, and the *Coach-maker's International Journal*— founded in 1865 and known by 1873 as *The Carriage Monthly*—carried articles that dwelt lovingly on the details of construction and decorating.

Collected by many "buggy nuts" in addition to the vehicles themselves, these journals can be studied at the Library of Congress and the Patent Office in Washington, D.C., and the public libraries in St. Louis and Detroit. They yield valuable nuggets on just how the Brewster or Studebaker or Kimball company built an axle, set a spring or achieved the luxuriously smooth finishes that made their carriages the satisfying displays of craftsmanship that they are.

For related material see the articles on Automobilia, Bicycles, Cars, Farm Machinery and Fire-Fighting Equipment in separate volumes of this encyclopedia.

A Goddard buggy, named for its designer, Boston carriage maker Thomas Goddard, has a convertible leather top. The buggies were often used by late-19th Century doctors to make their rounds.

A small pony-sailor wagon of 1900 seats two. The word pony in the name indicates that the carriage could be drawn by an animal smaller than a horse. Why the word sailor appeared in the name is no longer known.

This handsome 1910 surrey retains its original "fringe on top." An American design, the surrey was a four-passenger vehicle ideal for family picnics and other fair-weather outings.

A Jenny Lind buggy, named for the 19th Century singer and made about 1880, has a standing, or nonconvertible, top, rare in a buggy.

This relatively luxurious rig, built in New York state, had a covered driver's seat, and the windows were made to be raised and lowered.

This Bronson wagon, made of golden oak, was built by the well-known firm of Brewster & Company around 1901. It accommodated four passengers.

A phaeton made by Brewster & Company for city driving in 1898 accommodated a driver, one passenger and a servant who rode on the rumble seat.

Displaying the meticulous coachwork for which Brewster & Company was known, this carriage, called a basket vis-à-vis, was built in 1900. The name, French

for face to face, refers to the way that the occupants sat while a coachman up front drove. The body and fenders are willow basketwork woven over an iron frame.

Elegance and formality in the lines of a mid-1800s victoria, a coachman-driven town carriage for the well to do, were the pride of William D. Rogers, Philadelphia's leading carriage maker.

The Brewster-made brougham shown here originally cost $1,450, a steep price in 1890. Heavy, enclosed vehicles driven by coachmen, broughams were the top of the line among town carriages.

One of the largest private carriages designed, the park drag resembles a public stagecoach. This one, built in 1870 by the Paris firm Million

Guiet, seated 12 passengers on top and four servants inside. Managing its four horses allowed the driver to show off his equestrian skill.

Options for Carriages

Many collectors limit themselves to the accessories associated with horse-drawn carriages. The collectibles, which include foot warmers, jacks, coach horns and baskets used to hold canes and umbrellas, are much sought after. Perhaps the most popular collectible accessory is the carriage lamp. Because of their size (some are as high as 40 inches), ornate lamps that were fitted to hearses are especially sought after as impressive front-door ornaments. Round-lens lamps were often used on sporting or country vehicles, while more formal carriages frequently were equipped with fixtures that had square lenses. Carriage foot warmers come in a variety of types. One kind is made of tin overlaid with carpeting; a small drawer holds lighted coals. Another one is simply a block of soapstone, which retains heat very efficiently; it could be preheated in a fireplace before being placed in a carriage. A fur-lined foot warmer, like the one at right, was used like a muff for the feet.

A foot warmer of the 1890s is lined with raccoon fur. It served a dual purpose: closed, it kept a lady's feet toasty; when the tooled Moroccan-leather top was opened, it revealed a hidden jewel box.

The carriage lamps at left, 18 inches tall, are black japanned tin with silver-plated reflecting surfaces. These lamps were made in the late 19th Century in New Haven, Connecticut, by C. Cowles & Company.

A wagon jack, made of hardwood, stands 3 feet tall. A carriage owner or groom could fit its serrated edge to axles of various heights, use the lever to lift the carriage and grease the axles and wheel bearings.

The device fitted over the wheel rim at right is called a basket fender or wicker wheel guard. A gentleman would place it over the wheel when a lady was entering the carriage to protect her skirt from mud.

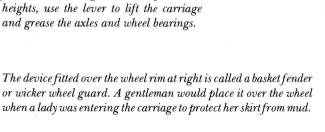

A useful sporting vehicle was the stubby 1890s carriage known as a shooting break, which carried retrievers in its boxlike body. In this photograph the wicker basket on the side holds a long brass coach horn instead of the umbrellas and walking sticks it was designed for.

The body of this two-wheeled dogcart, made in London in 1867 for driving to the fox hunt, can accommodate a couple of foxhounds.

A sulky of the 1850s, its driver's seat perched between the wheels, is a forerunner of the light two-wheeled rigs used in harness racing today.

This 1868 peddler's wagon, driven on rural New Hampshire roads for 20 or 30 years, has compartments and drawers where the itinerant merchant kept pins, buttons and other wares.

Deliveries in and around West Falmouth, Maine, kept this dairy wagon rolling from 1900 to 1920. The collector was able to restore it through a painstaking search for missing original parts.

A hearse retains the silver-trimmed, fringed drapery, mahogany interior and handsome original lamps of the 1880s. The wooden finials on top are carved to resemble plumes. Because not every collector wants one, a fine hearse can be a bargain.

A graceful sleigh made by French Carriage Company of Boston in the late 1800s is a vis-à-vis, still equipped with its original wool upholstery.

Usually painted in brilliant colors to show up against the snow, sleighs like this one are less expensive than carriages of the same body size.

MUSEUMS
The Carriage Museum at
The Museums at Stony Brook
Stony Brook, New York 11790

Greenfield Village and Henry Ford Museum
Dearborn, Michigan 48121

Horseshoe Barn at The Shelburne Museum, Inc.
Shelburne, Vermont 05482

Morven Park Carriage Museum
Westmoreland Davis Memorial Foundation, Inc.
Leesburg, Virginia 22075

National Museum of History and Technology
Smithsonian Institution
Washington, D.C. 20560

COLLECTORS ORGANIZATIONS
The American Driving Society
339 Warburton Avenue

Hastings-on-Hudson, New York 10706

The Carriage Association of America, Inc.
P.O. Box 3788
Portland, Maine 04104

PERIODICALS
The Carriage Journal, P.O. Box 3788, Portland, Maine 04104

BOOKS
Berkebile, Don H., ed., *American Carriages, Sleighs, Sulkies and Carts.* Dover Publications, Inc., 1977.

Berkebile, Don H., *Carriage Terminology: An Historical Dictionary.* Smithsonian Institution Press, 1978.

Tarr, László, *The History of the Carriage.* Arco Publishing Company, Inc., 1969.

Watney, Marylian, *The Elegant Carriage.* J. A. Allen & Co. Ltd., 1961.